cushions
quilts & throws

Lucinda Ganderton and Lucy Berridge

with photography by Sandra Lane

RYLAND
PETERS
& SMALL
LONDON   NEW YORK

Text and projects by Lucinda Ganderton
Stylist Lucy Berridge
Illustrator Lizzie Sanders

First published in 2003
This revised paperback edition published
in 2008 in the UK
by Ryland Peters & Small
20–21 Jockey's Fields
London WC1R 4BW
and in the USA
by Ryland Peters & Small, Inc.
519 Broadway
5th Floor
New York, NY 10012

www.rylandpeters.com
10 9 8 7 6 5 4 3 2 1

Text © Lucinda Ganderton 2003, 2008
Design and photographs
© Ryland Peters & Small 2003, 2008

ISBN: 978-1-84597-6-996

PRINTED IN CHINA

important note:
Measurements for the projects in this book are
given in metric and imperial. Conversions are
not exact. Always follow either the metric or the
imperial measurements when making up a
project and not a mixture of both.

A CIP record for this book is available
from the British Library.

The hardcover edition of this
book was cataloged as follows by
the Library of Congress:

Ganderton, Lucinda.
  Pillows and throws / Lucinda
Ganderton and Lucy Berridge ; with
photography by Sandra Lane.
    p. cm.
Includes index.
  ISBN 1-84172-476-9
  1. Cushions. 2. Throws (Coverlets)
I. Berridge, Lucy. II. Title.
TT410.G36 2003
  746.9'5--dc21

                    2003009169

contents

OPPOSITE, TOP LEFT Beds can be dressed with extra pillows and throws to make them look attractive during the daytime.

OPPOSITE, TOP RIGHT Patchwork is one of the easiest needlecrafts to master. Be inspired by this gorgeous cushion cover – see how to make it on page 74.

OPPOSITE, BELOW One-off cushions, like this original trio, can be appreciated as pieces of textile art rather than mere soft furnishing accessories.

LEFT Utilitarian mattress ticking has risen from its humble origins to become a sought after furnishing fabric.

introduction

It may have become something of a truism, but a scattering of cushions and a well-placed throw or blanket really can transform an ordinary room into an inspiring interior. This old decorating principle has been updated by a new generation of designers who are using soft furnishings in the same way as fashion accessories – as a stylish means of creating a strong impact and a fresh, new look.

Cushions, pillows and throws can be incorporated into the home in myriad ways. With a little imagination, you can enhance classic furniture with a carefully chosen cushion or disguise less-than-perfect upholstery by draping a luxurious cashmere shawl over an old sofa, while layers of folded eiderdowns add a welcoming look to a plain bed.

This book brings together an exciting array of contemporary living and sleeping spaces. Grouped into nine design themes – ranging from cool neutral and modern retro to the vintage florals of shabby chic – they all show just how easy it is to add instant style and character to your surroundings, whatever your personal taste.

Whether you long for zen-like serenity
or prefer more sensual surroundings,
look to nature for inspiration. Rather
than gardens or woodland, visualize vast
open spaces, such as deserts, ice-floes
and mountains and the colours that define
them, and you will find natural shades and
textures that adapt to any style of interior.

neutrals & naturals

OPPOSITE These linen cushion covers are recycled from vintage sheets which were hand embroidered with their owners' initials, following the elaborate satin stitch templates given in specially produced alphabet pattern books.

LEFT A glass-topped table and large mirror heighten the feeling of airiness in this bright living room.

RIGHT The integral texture of this cream fabric, which incorporates regularly spaced tufts, avoids the need for any additional fringing, tassels or piping/cording. Its intricate weave could be imitated by stitching small bundles of thread on to a plain background.

BELOW A simple row of alternating dark and light square cushions gives a neat and orderly appearance to a low-level seating arrangement.

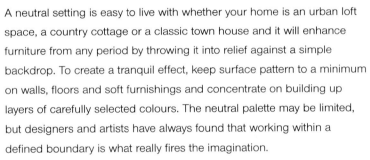

A neutral setting is easy to live with whether your home is an urban loft space, a country cottage or a classic town house and it will enhance furniture from any period by throwing it into relief against a simple backdrop. To create a tranquil effect, keep surface pattern to a minimum on walls, floors and soft furnishings and concentrate on building up layers of carefully selected colours. The neutral palette may be limited, but designers and artists have always found that working within a defined boundary is what really fires the imagination.

The neutral colours that occur together in the natural world will always complement each other without clashing. These fall into two distinct groupings: the warm tones of polished wood, ivory, straw and amber and the cooler greys and blues of frost, slate and pewter. Depending on the degree of impact you wish to create, you can mix together warm and cold colours from the two groups; limit your choice to just two or three closely related pale colours for a restful atmosphere, or integrate lights and darks in similar tones for more drama.

Remember, however, that some variation of tone – and it only need be a single accent – is necessary in even the most neutral of settings. Introduce a few well-chosen accessories to add blocks of extra colour: a cream velvet cushion set against a dark sofa or a rich brown throw to anchor a pale linen chair will provide just enough contrast to give

OPPOSITE A mahogany four-poster bed with fluted pillars becomes a calm sanctuary when dressed with pure white cotton and linen and piled high with pillows and monogrammed cushions.

ABOVE LEFT Winged armchairs can appear ponderous, but a loose linen cover gives this one a refreshing sense of lightness. Painters' dust sheets are a good source of fabric for similar covers.

TOP A casually folded throw draped over the arm of a chair or sofa can make even the most formal seating appear welcoming.

ABOVE In an inspired pairing of natural textures, this dove-grey suede cushion is bordered with curly fake sheepskin.

ABOVE These chunky woollen cushion covers, reminiscent of *The Borrowers*, are worked in an over-sized stocking stitch. They are finished off along the top and bottom edges with a simple, nubbly fringe made from the same yarn.

ABOVE RIGHT Pattern used in a neutral setting works best when it is either very small or very large. This textured sunburst appliqué makes a bold graphic statement on a square pillowcase.

OPPOSITE Cushions knitted from thick cream yarn, a padded and quilted throw made from unbleached linen, and two crisp white pillows give an unmistakably contemporary look to a period bed. The contrasting textures are united by the use of a limited selection of gentle, natural colours.

character and life to a room. Always include an element of pure white somewhere within a neutral or monochrome scheme – gloss paint on a window frame and skirting, crisp cotton sheets on an antique bed or a linen slip cover for a battered armchair – to prevent the room becoming too bland and lifeless.

The range of textures within the family of natural fabrics is enormous. In addition to woollen blankets, cotton pillowcases and embroidered bed linen, look for water-marked moirés, eyelet laces and luxurious silks, satins and velvets. If you would like to introduce a discreet element of pattern, single-colour weaves are a good choice. Jacquards and damasks come in a range of stripes, as well as florals and geometrics, which combine smooth and shiny mercerized threads to produce an almost three-dimensional effect. To fit in with the overall scheme, designs that feature two or more colours should be either boldly over-sized and graphic or on such a small scale that they are reduced to a simple texture.

Advances in weaving looms and knitting machines mean that designers can now bring together different textures and fibres as never before, and the latest fabrics are consequently excitingly tactile.

They give a new twist to traditional furniture and work especially well with contemporary sofas and chairs: even a modernist couch sometimes needs a squashy, appealing cushion to relax into, while a cable-knit throw will increase the comfort level of even the most welcoming bed.

Leather – another natural product – has long been a favourite material for living room furniture; it looks better with age, is easy to clean, is pretty much child- and pet-proof and can prove to be an investment in the long term. A button-back chesterfield or a wood-framed Robin Day sofa will last for years and, by adding different throws and cushions, they can be easily adapted to suit changes in style as the room evolves.

In addition to real hides, textile technology has produced a wide selection of faux leathers and furs (cheaper, kinder and easier to clean than the real thing) which includes suedes, mock crocodile, camp zebra stripes and scaly snakeskins. Used in moderation, these will all add an element of textural quality to a neutral room. Hunt down other unusual materials with contrasting surfaces and place them together to accentuate their individual characteristics: a heavy

OPPOSITE Natural textures and found objects from the countryside – bare floor boards, a carved wooden overmantel, a willow log basket and a vase of cow parsley seed heads – are reflected in the soft furnishings of this timeless and individual living room.

LEFT This fringed and felted throw is made to stand out by its raised surface decoration.

ABOVE A linen panel, draped casually over a ladder-back chair, emphasizes the delicate embroidery on the bag.

looped fringing on a glazed cotton cushion, a shaggy faux-sheepskin border on a challis throw or a silk bolster edged with a fringe of feathers or clear glass beads would all look stunning.

The play of light – both natural and artificial – is an essential quality in any room, and one which is often overlooked. It is especially important in a room where the background is neutral and the fabrics textured. Different textures absorb light in different ways: reflective fabrics, like satins and glazed chintz, bounce light back into a room, while the denser surface of wools and velvets will soak it up and appear darker. Lighting should be planned to enhance the soft furnishings with spotlights, mirrors and carefully positioned table lamps to help keep the space animated and bright. Interior designers classify crystal, silver and gilt as neutrals, as they too blend into any scheme. An ornate gold picture frame, chandelier, mirrored table or a tall pier glass will all increase the light where necessary.

Plain walls in lustrous eggshell or matte finish are a good foil for natural and neutral fabrics. Farrow and Ball and Fired Earth both have a comprehensive range of off-white paint colours for wood, walls and floors. Some of the shades are new, others historic – based on samples uncovered in old houses. They cover the full range of shades from cool blue-whites, through to lime washes, clotted creams, taupes, putties and greige. Continue the natural theme through to the floor to complete the look. Wood strip, laminates or bare pine boards which have been sanded, stained or painted finish off the room perfectly.

If you prefer a degree of comfort underfoot you can add large rugs, which do for floors what throws do for beds and sofas. The once ubiquitous coir matting is now being superseded by innovative carpet weaves in 100 percent wool. The newest heavily textured ridged and herringbone patterns have the same natural quality as coir but are warmer and more durable.

OPPOSITE, LEFT A loose-fitting cover, like the white slip on this sofa, looks much more relaxed than conventional upholstery. The interlined curtains, a ribbed throw and the palest cushions continue the neutral colour theme in an informal setting.

OPPOSITE, RIGHT The deeply textured cushion cover – an open grid over a puckered inner layer – sits happily on the buttoned padding of a twentieth-century classic chair.

LEFT Contrasting lengths of cream and unbleached linen were used to make this simple throw: see how on the following pages.

ABOVE Drawn thread work is usually found on fine napkins and dainty table mats. Here the technique is used on a much larger scale.

neutrals & naturals 17

linen throw
I made this throw from two remnants of antique linen which were discovered during a house clearance in the south of France. The heavy cloth has a unique hand-woven texture and needed very little in the way of embellishment. To give it a new life I simply worked four bands of ladder hem stitch across the width of the centre panel and fringed the edges to reveal the distinctive quality of the thread.

I Make a 2.5cm (1in) fringe along the short edges of all three pieces of linen by pulling the threads away from the fabric one at a time. Use the point of a tapestry needle to separate the fibres if they do not come apart easily. Fringe one long edge of one of the light strips in the same way.

2 Neaten/finish one long edge of the other light strip with a narrow double hem. Pin and tack/baste it in place and stitch down by hand or machine.

3 To mark the positions of the drawn thread foundations for the hem stitch, make four small snips along one long edge of the dark linen rectangle 25, 43, 70 and 78cm (10, 17, 28 and 31in) along from the bottom left corner.

MATERIALS AND EQUIPMENT

coarse weave linen in two shades
small tapestry needle
matching sewing thread
1 skein of white stranded embroidery cotton/floss
sewing kit
sewing machine

CUTTING OUT

from the dark linen:
one 53 x 105cm
(21 x 41in) rectangle

from the light linen:
one 35 x 105cm (14 x 41in) rectangle
one 25 x 105cm (10 x 41in) rectangle

4 Using the snipped edges as a guide, pull out threads across the width of the fabric so that each band is between 1–2.5cm (½–1in) wide. You may find it helps to snip them as you work, and again you can use a blunt needle to ease them apart.

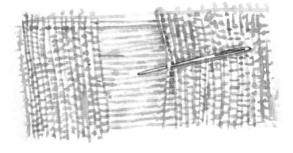

5 Thread the tapestry needle with a length of stranded cotton/floss. Starting 2.5cm (1in) from the left-hand edge of the first open band work a few short running stitches towards the edge of the fabric, close to the open band. These will anchor the cotton/floss and be concealed by the hem stitch. To work the hem stitch, bring the needle up at the far left, then slide it behind the first eight threads.

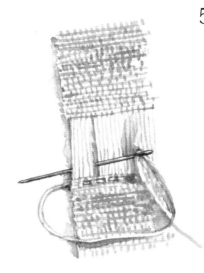

6 Insert the needle to the right of the threads and bring the point out about 3mm (⅛in) down from the edge. Pull the cotton/floss gently to bunch the threads. Continue to the end, finishing off each length of cotton/floss with several short running stitches. Repeat on the other side of the open band, working over the same groups of threads to make a series of 'rungs'.

7 Pin and tack/baste the raw edge of one light strip to one long edge of the dark panel, leaving a 2cm (¾in) seam allowance and finish with a flat fell seam (see page 114).

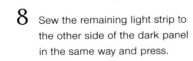

8 Sew the remaining light strip to the other side of the dark panel in the same way and press.

These are the most opulent fabrics of all — gloriously colourful, textured and extravagantly patterned. Used with discretion, they will bring a touch of luxury to any room — a single damask cushion or an artfully displayed velvet throw is all that is needed to make the transformation from simple to sumptuous.

silk & velvet

OPPOSITE A silvery velvet cushion, which takes its colour from the padded footstool, is the accent needed to lift the flamboyant purple of the two sofas.

LEFT These pillow-sized brocade cushions would make a stunning accessory in a room of any period, although the setting here is undeniably modern.

RIGHT A wooden settle is softened by the addition of a gleaming grey silk throw edged with a deep black fringe and two coordinating square cushions.

BELOW There is a fusion of luxurious textures in this sophisticated living room, with plush velvets and shiny satins meeting smooth leather and cotton fringing.

Silk has always been highly prized by dressmakers and interior designers. Originally cultivated and woven in China more than 4,000 years ago, traders first brought bales of fabric to the West along the hazardous Silk Route. Silk thread is spun from the inner fibres that line the cocoons of the silk moth and over the years it has been woven into various types of cloth for garments and furnishings. Many of these fabrics have evocative names; brocatelle, gossamer, bombazine, baldachin, holosericum and the intriguing rumchunder.

Despite its fragile appearance, silk is deceptively strong – it has been used to make parachutes as well as wedding gowns. The fibres are sometimes blended with linen or wool to create different surface textures and patterned weaves. Silk absorbs dye well, giving a great depth of tone and colour to the finished fabric: jewel-like turquoise and tangerine, lime green, purple and shocking pink are as popular as neutral off-white, rich cream, stone and chocolate.

Velvet is made from silk, cotton, wool or any mixture of those three fibres. Its softness comes from the thick cut pile, which can be left plain or decorated. Devoré velvet is screen printed in a chemical process that literally 'eats away' the pile, leaving a heavily textured design, while Utrecht velvet is passed between heated rollers to stamp in a design. Plain velvet has an understated elegance that fits into most interiors and is often used to upholster chairs and sofas, while the figured versions are most effective when used in combination with other fabrics.

ABOVE The scalloped border of this deeply textured pillow echoes the curved lines of the small sofa upon which it rests.

RIGHT The braid that encircles this bolster serves the double purpose of adding decoration and disguising the seams. See how to make it overleaf.

OPPOSITE Sugared almond colours in the softest pinks, pistachios and lilacs give this room a look that is undeniably feminine, without being at all frilly. An embroidered silk shawl doubles up as a throw and the square cushion is simply put together by stitching a length of a fringed, striped fabric on to a pink velvet cover.

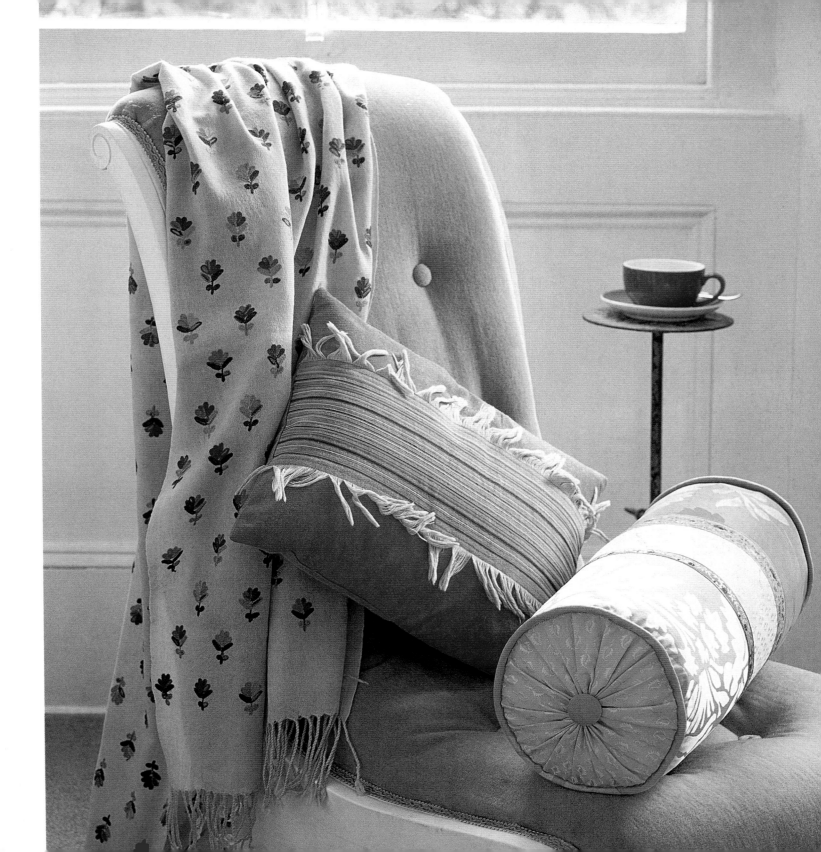

sugared almond bolster

This silk bolster is an exercise in unashamed extravagance, guaranteed to add a touch of boudoir-like luxury to even the most ordinary surroundings. The lustrous brocade cover is piped/corded and gathered at each end and trimmed with matching buttons. It is cut slightly smaller than the feather-filled cushion pad/form which gives it a satisfyingly plump, upholstered appearance.

MATERIALS AND EQUIPMENT

silk brocade in dark turquoise, lime green and pink

matching sewing thread

two 58cm (23in) lengths of woven ribbon or braid

116cm (46in) medium piping cord

45 x 16cm (18 x 6½in) bolster pad/form

two 3cm (1¼in) self-cover buttons

sewing kit

sewing machine

CUTTING OUT

for the main cover:

one 18 x 58cm (7 x 23in) strip of dark turquoise silk

one 14 x 58cm (5½ x 23in) strip of lime-green silk

one 23 x 58cm (9 x 23in) strip of pink silk

for the gathered ends:

two 11 x 58cm (4½ x 23in) strips of lime-green silk

for the piping/cording:

two 5 x 58cm (2 x 23in) bias strips of pink silk cut with diagonal ends sloping in the same direction

1 With right sides together, pin and tack/baste the three strips of silk together to make the cover. Machine stitch, leaving a seam allowance of 1cm (⅜in). Press the seams open.

2 Pin the two lengths of braid to the right side, covering the seams. Tack/baste and machine stitch down. Start each line of stitching from the same end to prevent the braid puckering.

3 With right sides together, pin, tack/baste and machine stitch the shorter edges to make a cylinder, leaving a seam allowance of 1cm (⅜in). Press the seam open and turn the cover right side out.

4 Slip stitch and bind the ends of one length of piping cord together to form a loop (see page 116), overlapping them by 1cm (½in).

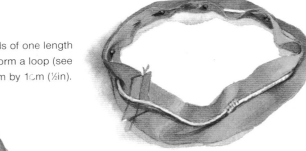

5 Sew the diagonal ends of one bias strip with right sides together, leaving a seam allowance of 1cm (½in) and press the seam open. Fold the fabric loop over the cord with wrong sides together and pin and tack/baste close to the cord. Make the second round of piping/cording in the same way.

6 Matching the raw edges and lining up the seams, pin and tack/baste a round of piping/cording around each end of the main cover.

7 With right sides together, join the short edges of an end strip and press the seam open. Make a 1cm (½in) hem around one edge.

8 With right sides and raw edges together, slip the end loop over one end of the main cover, covering the piping/cording and lining up the seams. Pin and tack/baste, then machine stitch in place using a zipper foot so that the seam lies close to the piping/cording. Do the same at the other end with the other end strip.

9 Insert the bolster pad/form and, using a double length of thread, work a round of long running stitches around one opening just outside the seam line. Pull the thread up gently to form evenly spaced gathers. Tuck the hem inside the cover and knot off tightly. Finish off the other end in the same way.

10 Following the manufacturer's instructions, cover the buttons with offcuts of pink fabric and sew them in place at each end. When the cover needs to be cleaned, cut off the buttons, snip the thread and remove the pad/form.

THIS PAGE A selection of Chinese-style brocades in duck-egg blue, rich cream and coffee has been used to make this trio of silk cushions. The colours complement each other perfectly, while the blend of floral designs, stripes and woven geometrics is both harmonious and pleasing.

OPPOSITE RIGHT AND LEFT Fine silk veiling and black leather may not be an obvious fusion of fabrics but the result is sensational. The flower motifs give weight to the delicate ground fabric, creating a striking throw which hangs gracefully over the arm of a large, comfortable sofa. See how it is made on the next page.

Silk damask – originally manufactured in Damascus, from where it takes its name, and later in Europe as production became more widespread – is a single-colour fabric with a matte pattern woven into a shiny satin background. It is reversible which makes it ideal for lightweight throws and unlined curtains. Some of the flowing designs are based on floral, arabesque and foliage patterns which date back to the Renaissance, sometimes even earlier, but innovative designers are always creating exciting new fabrics. Brocades are multicoloured weaves which come in many patterns, from Chinoiserie blossoms and subtly hued florals to the latest geometrics. Despite the historical connotations of these opulent fabrics, their inherent style defies changing trends in both fashion and interior design and they work equally well as part of formal and informal contemporary interiors.

Exploited on a grand scale, such extravagant materials can look theatrical and dramatic, but unless you live in a stately home or are recreating a historic look, they can be a bit overwhelming. However, by contrasting them with simpler textures, you can counterbalance the effect. The luminous texture of silk or a figured velvet appears even more intense when juxtaposed with an expanse of plain colour or set against a neutral background. On a more prosaic note, luxurious fabrics often have price tags to match, but remnants and large swatches can easily be incorporated into cushion covers or bolsters. Furnishing shops sometimes sell off sample books which can be used for patchwork throws or small cushion covers.

Damask and brocade have traditionally been used for curtains and upholstery, but fashion fabrics are increasingly being used in every aspect of home furnishing. Dressmaking materials will not stand up to hard wear but are often decorative and distinctive. Sari fabrics are a favourite, while fine nets can be used to make delicate throws. Taffeta, with its high sheen, has made the transition from ball gown to cushion cover and sheer organza can be used at a window or to make a tie-on cover for a cushion made from a heavier material.

ethereal throw

A stunning combination of white net and black leather, this throw has an ethereal quality which is quite unique – the flower and leaf silhouettes almost appear to float across the surface of the silk. Its creator, textile artist Karen Nichol, works primarily with leading fashion designers and her true understanding of fabrics is revealed in the pairing of such contrasting weights and textures.

MATERIALS AND EQUIPMENT

iron-on bonding web
sharp pencil
approximately 50 x 100cm (20 x 40in)
thin black leather
old sheet
140cm (55in) square of silk net
sewing kit

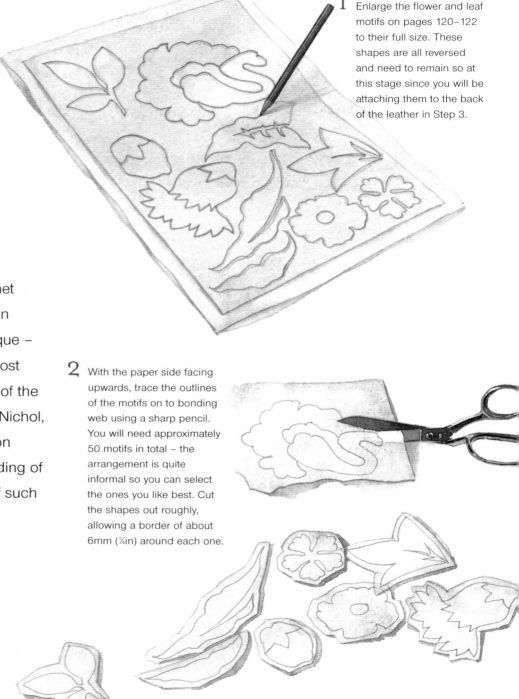

1 Enlarge the flower and leaf motifs on pages 120–122 to their full size. These shapes are all reversed and need to remain so at this stage since you will be attaching them to the back of the leather in Step 3.

2 With the paper side facing upwards, trace the outlines of the motifs on to bonding web using a sharp pencil. You will need approximately 50 motifs in total – the arrangement is quite informal so you can select the ones you like best. Cut the shapes out roughly, allowing a border of about 6mm (¼in) around each one.

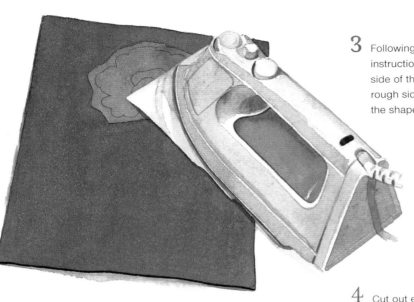

3 Following the manufacturer's instructions, iron the adhesive side of the bonding web on to the rough side of the leather, fitting the shapes together like a jigsaw.

4 Cut out each shape carefully, following the pencil lines. Where a motif has several elements, cut out just around the main outline at this stage.

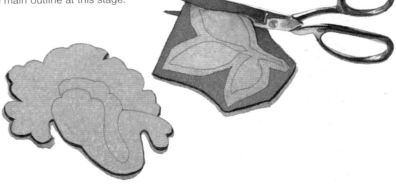

5 Fold the old sheet in half and lay it out flat on a hard surface: a tiled or wooden floor is ideal. Put the net on top of the sheet and arrange 9–12 motifs, leather side up, in each corner of the net. Group them loosely to form a random pattern.

6 When you are satisfied with the arrangement, cut out the separate pieces of the complex motifs and space them out. Peel off the backing paper from the motifs, then, following the manufacturer's instructions, iron each shape in place using a pressing cloth to protect the surface of the leather.

Cashmere and woollen yarns have been knitted and woven into some of the most tactile and luxurious fabrics around. So when it comes to keeping warm and creating a welcoming atmosphere, fluffy blankets, wool throws and big soft cushions are the obvious choice.

cashmere & wool

OPPOSITE A modest blanket fringe takes on a new importance as the main feature of this woollen cushion.

LEFT This lustrous pashmina throw is framed by a deep border of toning satin.

RIGHT Iridescent mother-of-pearl buttons serve as fastenings for a knitted cover.

BELOW LEFT This feminine lilac cushion cover features a knotted lacy fringe and exquisite hand embroidery.

BELOW RIGHT A mixture of grey fibres gives an attractive marl finish to this woollen throw, which complements the stitching and satin braid.

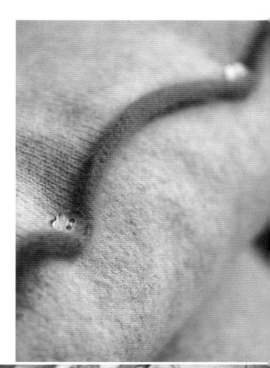

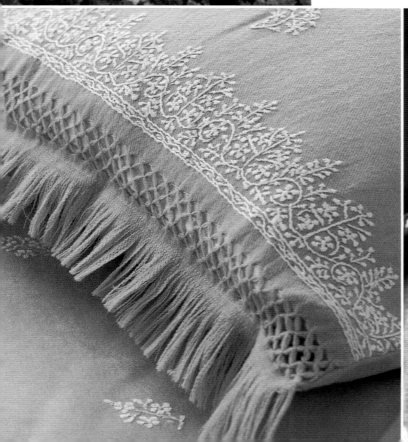

The contemporary interior should, above all else, be comfortable and relaxing. We need to feel at ease in our homes, and the soft and welcoming fabrics made from wool and cashmere are becoming an increasingly popular option for dressing not just ourselves but our living spaces and bedrooms, too. These fabrics are immensely versatile – as natural fibres, they give a warm glow in winter but are cool in summer; they are subtle enough for a neutral scheme or jewel-bright if you prefer stronger colours; and they are surprisingly easy to look after and clean.

Cashmere has to be the world's most sumptuous fibre. Its qualities have always been valued as unique and it was favoured by royalty and emperors from Queen Victoria to Napoleon (who presented his Empress with a dozen of the finest cashmere shawls). Like pashmina, cashmere is gathered from a goat native to the Gobi desert. In such inclement surroundings the creatures developed a double fleece – the outer layer is thick and coarse to provide a defence against bitter winds and the undercoat offers extra insulation. This fine second layer is shed naturally and the fibres are combed out and collected by hand. The llama-like alpaca has a similar soft coat, which is becoming an increasingly popular ingredient in woven fabrics.

The fleece of the more humble sheep is sheared annually to give a fibre that is resilient and warm – after all, it too was designed to keep the original wearers protected from the elements. The wool from each different breed of sheep has its own colour and characteristics: that of the merino sheep, originally from Spain, is

ABOVE AND LEFT The appeal of these two woollen cushions lies in the inventive combination of texture, colour and detail – a heavenly blue velvet ribbon on palest cream and a pair of delicious felt cherries on an apple green background.

OPPOSITE A fringed blanket, a huge square cushion and a mattress cushion, all woven from undyed wool, together show just how wide the span of natural colours and shades can be.

THIS PAGE An all-white space does not have to be austere. Here, a textured rug and a cashmere throw soften bare floorboards and a sleek sofa, while paintings and sumptuous cushions introduce a touch of warm, golden colour.

OPPOSITE LEFT The unexpected pairing of honey-toned cashmere and faux fur diamonds gives a sensuous feeling to the coordinating throw and cushion.

OPPOSITE RIGHT Satin and the finest cashmere make an irresistible combination which just invites you to curl up in the corner of the sofa.

especially soft while the hardy Shetland, which evolved on the windswept Scottish islands, has a downy under layer which is spun into an extremely fine yarn.

Like silk, wool dyes particularly well producing rich, clear hues. However, left in its raw state the colours range from palest cream, through fawn and grey to beige and the chocolate brown of the Jacob sheep. These colours blend together harmoniously, giving a naturally pleasing result. The classic Shetland pullovers were knitted in intricate snowflake and diamond patterns using only undyed yarns, and the same colours are also made into wonderful woven fabrics for clothing and blankets.

Most of us have a travel rug somewhere, in the boot of the car ready for a family picnic or tucked over the spare bed. Woven in tartan, plaid or harlequin squares, these hard-wearing blankets are finished off with chunky fringes and the older ones often feature interesting labels. Lighter weight waffle-weave and cellular blankets are good for children and for warm nights, and can be layered when the weather turns cooler.

However, blankets are not just for use on beds. Manufacturers are expanding their collections to include innovative colours and designs which now come in all sizes – from the tiniest squares to tuck round sleeping babies, to super-king rectangles almost three metres wide. Small ones can be used as throws while larger versions can be draped over a sofa to disguise shabby or outmoded upholstery. Wide ones will, of course, double up as bedspreads. Woollen blankets appeal to our nesting instinct – a long, cold winter's evening can happily be spent wrapped up in one, while watching a favourite film.

LEFT A corona of gauzy fabric hung at ceiling height will frame a bed to create a strong visual feature against plain walls. Casually draped pashminas and a pile of pretty cushions continue the romantic boudoir theme.

BELOW Lace-like embroidery, worked in a scrolling flower and foliage pattern, adds delicacy to a finely woven pillow cover.

OPPOSITE Throws and pillowslips can easily be swapped around to change the appearance of a room. In this sun drenched bedroom, summery pastels – light sage and cool lilac – have been used to introduce muted colour into an otherwise neutral scheme. A light embroidered shawl covers the cream duvet and complementary pillows complete the look.

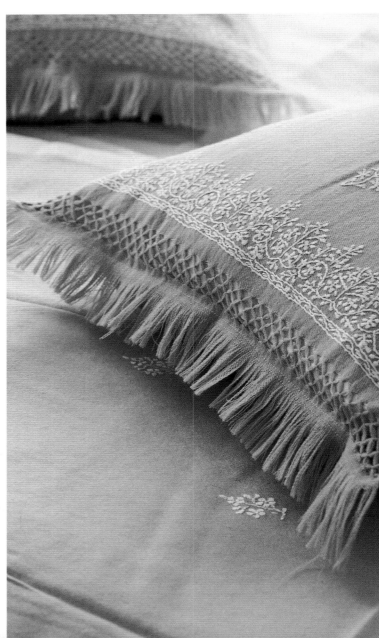

The newest bedspreads and knitted throws are essentially fashion accessories for the home. Designer Ralph Lauren, along with Italian knitwear specialists Etro and Missoni, is expanding the market with an array of beautiful throws and blankets. One-off craft weavers, creating fabulous fabrics on a domestic scale, are a long way from their old homespun image and long-established woollen mills, like Melin Tregwynt, have come up with exciting, fresh ideas by reinterpreting the traditional Welsh double-weave patterns. Now nursing shawls and products from this family-owned mill can be found in the hippest hotels.

Knit and weave manufacturers are increasingly including other home accessories in their ranges, especially coordinating cushions. It is, however, very easy to make your own cushion covers from old blankets, a length of tweed or any other woven wool fabric. Follow the instructions for the basic cushion on page 117 and stitch the opening together by hand. Wool is too thick for fiddly details like piping/cording or a zip fastening, but a simple cushion can be embellished with extra decoration such as a row of buttons. If you are feeling adventurous, you can recycle the main part of an old sweater into a rectangular cushion cover. Turn the garment inside out and tack/baste both layers together across the body, just below the level of the sleeves. Machine stitch along this line using a stitch for

BELOW The paisley motif featured on this sumptuous cushion was introduced to the Europeans in the eighteenth century, when merchants first imported magnificent cashmere shawls from India. Highly sought after by ladies of fashion, the finest took several years to weave and cost a small fortune. Enterprising manufacturers in Paisley eventually copied the patterns on jacquard looms and so the swirling Eastern patterns became known by the name of a Scottish mill town.

RIGHT The raw edges of woollen blankets have always been bound and neatened/finished with satin ribbon, the two contrasting textures enhancing each other perfectly. This finish is given a new elegance on a pashmina throw.

OPPOSITE Reworked from an old embroidered shawl that has been backed with silk and trimmed with braid, this throw is straightforward to make and requires only basic sewing skills: see instructions on page 40.

jersey, then cut away the surplus material, neaten/finish the seam and turn the garment right side out. Insert the cushion pad/form, then slip stitch along the hem of the open side to finish off.

You need not worry too much about cleaning wool or cashmere. Heat and agitation are what cause the fibres to shrink and felt, so if you keep to cool water and avoid rubbing, your treasured woollens (including jumpers and cardigans) will be safe. Most washing machines have a special low-temperature wool cycle which has a slow action, but you can also wash woollens by hand. Fill a sink or bath with lukewarm water and add some mild soap flakes. Soak the items for about one hour then change the water. Drain and squeeze gently, without twisting. Dry on a washing line or indoors over a shower curtain rail/rod or lay flat on a towel.

Forget any preconceptions you may have about wool being itchy or scratchy. New blends, which may incorporate camel hair or linen, and wool/silk mixes, along with special finishing processes, mean that it is now softer to the touch than ever before and also easy to care for. The commonplace family blanket has been transformed into a luxury product.

wool and silk throw

This luxurious throw provides the perfect solution to the eternal quandary – what do you do with last season's fashion accessories? Here is one idea. French-born interior designer Laurent Bayard, whose eclectic sense of style is inspired by a passion for antiques and travel, rescued an embroidered shawl from the back of the wardrobe and transformed it into an object of desire, ready for a new life as an irresistible soft furnishing!

MATERIALS AND EQUIPMENT

silk fabric
embroidered woollen shawl
1cm (½in) wide gold ribbon
8cm (3in) wide geometric weave braid
3.5cm (1½in) wide floral braid
matching sewing thread
sewing kit

CUTTING OUT

for the backing:
1 rectangle silk, 1cm (½in) shorter and 8cm (3in) wider than the shawl (excluding fringe)

for the border:
each length measures twice the width of the shawl plus 5cm (2in)
4 lengths gold ribbon
2 lengths geometric braid
4 lengths floral braid

I Press under a 1cm (½in) turning along each long edge of the silk backing.

2 Lay the backing out on a large flat surface with the right side facing downwards. Place the shawl over the silk with the right side up, centring it so that there is a 3cm (1¼in) margin showing at each long edge and the short edges of the silk lie 6mm (¼in) from the fringes.

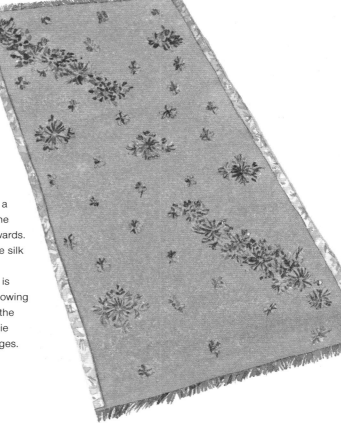

3 Keeping the fabric flat, pin the short edges together. Turn the long edges to the front and pin in place close to the fold. Tack/baste all four edges.

4 Sew the shawl and backing together along the fringed edges by hand, using running stitch. Slip stitch the long folded edges through both layers, using a thread to match the silk fabric.

5 Cut two lengths of gold ribbon measuring twice the width of the throw plus 3cm (1in). Leaving a 2cm (¾in) overlap at the end, pin the ribbon along one fringed edge, hiding the raw edge of the silk. Turn the throw over and pin the second half of the ribbon in place. Trim the ends of the ribbon to 6mm (¼in) and fold them under neatly. Tack/baste and machine stitch the ribbon close to the edges. Start each line of stitching from the same end so that the ribbon does not pucker.

6 Machine stitch the second length of gold ribbon along the centre of the geometric braid. Tack/baste, then machine stitch a length of floral braid to each edge of the geometric braid to make a wide band. Press under a 2cm (¾in) turning at one short end of the band.

7 Starting 1cm (½in) in from the long edge and 4cm (1½in) from the gold ribbon, pin both edges of the braid band across the width of the woollen side of the shawl. Turn over and continue pinning to the other side. Fold over the neatened/finished end to conceal the raw edges.

8 Tack/baste the braid in place and slip stitch through all three layers. Repeat Steps 5–7 at the other fringed end of the shawl to complete the throw.

Stripes — and checks, their natural cousins —
come in many guises: broad or narrow,
sombre or casual, grown-up or playful.
They are effective when used singly, but as
basic geometric designs they work very well
together, and they are versatile enough to
fit in with many different schemes.

stripes & checks

OPPOSITE Two large square pillows in windowpane check, a striped blanket and a chevron patterned bedcover together give a structured daytime look to a divan bed.

LEFT Padded mattress cushions, designed to soften hard seating, are portable and look as much at home indoors as they do on garden furniture.

RIGHT These candy stripes, in narrow bands of blue and orange on pink, are exuberant and cheerful.

BELOW Flower prints and plaids make a happy partnership. A huge woollen blanket – a traditional pattern reworked in brighter colours – is piled high with large floral cushions for comfortable outdoor living on a summer's day.

There may be occasions when you wish to introduce a degree of surface pattern into a room without resorting to patterned prints, in which case stripes and checks – or a mixture of the two – could be the answer. The classic stripe is coming into its own as a design solution and variations on the theme can be seen on everything from Paul Smith carrier bags and haute couture gowns to the coolest walls and floors.

Designs featuring wide bands of colour in two contrasting tones will always seem formal, particularly when used on wallpaper or upholstery. These regency stripes feel calm and static, while narrow, multicoloured stripes are more lively and light-hearted. Very broad stripes in any mix of colours have an open-air, festive feel about them, suggesting old-fashioned shop awnings or tented marquees. Blue and white stripes inevitably have nautical associations, but seaside towns are full of all sorts of stripes: multicoloured deck chairs, red and white lighthouses, sticks of rock and flags. Traditional striped blazers, shirts and old school ties throw up gaudy or unexpectedly harmonious colour combinations. All of these looks can be adapted to interiors, and stripes can be used horizontally, vertically or diagonally for a dramatically different effect.

The thin stripes found on ticking have a functional appeal that can be either relaxed or formal, depending on the setting. This utilitarian cloth was originally used to cover mattresses and pillows, as the sturdy twill weave prevented any feathers working out. It is now recognized as a furnishing fabric in its own right and is used for cushions, loose covers and curtains. It will complement old fabrics and when mixed in with

OPPOSITE AND ABOVE LEFT A vibrant multicoloured stripe, used for both cushions and a throw, is counterbalanced by a plain throw with a toning border made from velvet ribbon. The stripes are all set horizontally to prevent the overall effect becoming too busy.

TOP RIGHT The futuristic lines of Ernest Race's Antelope chair are softened with a cushion and folded blanket.

ABOVE Stripes and checks, recycled from vivid knitted and woven fabrics, are patchworked together to make this individual woollen cushion.

rose-printed chintzes or other flower designs, it can often prevent the overall look becoming too fussy. Antique examples, including European mattress ticking in reds, creams and warm browns, or original blue and white French Vichy material, are much sought after. Even the smallest remnant can be utilized to make a cushion cover or cylindrical bolster. Designer Ian Mankin produces a range of new ticking in many different widths and colourways.

The most understated stripes of all can be found on brocades and other jacquard woven fabrics. These self stripes are the same colour but the texture of the weave alternates between a smooth satin finish and a matt surface. These, along with natural hued stripes, work well in neutral surroundings.

In simple terms, a check consists of two sets of stripes set at right angles to each other and interwoven to produce a grid. There are myriad permutations within the limitations of this woven format giving an immense variety of checks, both in pattern and mood. In design terminology, a check is strictly a design made up of even stripes which produce a regular square pattern; gingham is a good example. The squares in a windowpane check are outlined by thin lines and big lumberjack checks are known, not surprisingly, as buffaloes. Anything else, where the stripes are irregular, is a plaid.

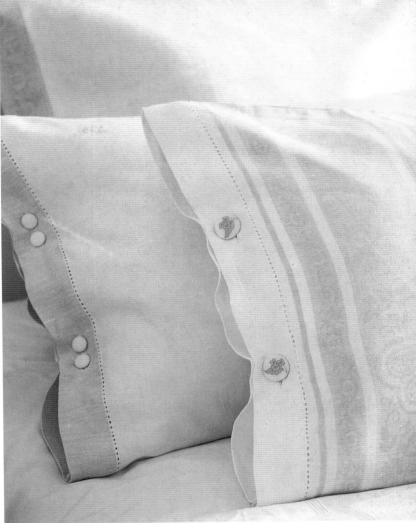

OPPOSITE A simple bedspread is all that is needed to cover up your bed during the daytime, but it can end up looking a little 'undressed'. By adding extra throws or quilts you can create a much more attractive, finished look, as in this comfortable room. A theme of stripes and flowers links the assortment of covers and linen used on the bed: a folded woollen blanket and a floral eiderdown lie across the foot of the bed on top of an antique quilt patterned with wide bands of roses.

LEFT Shell pink bands, themselves patterned with fine twill stripes, run along the border of this pillowcase. They are echoed by the line of open hem stitch and the raised embroidery on the covered button.

ABOVE Sometimes just a single stripe, like the one which edges the centre pillow, is enough to give character and distinction to a fabric.

mattress cushion

These chunky cushions, like scaled-down versions of a traditional mattress, make for comfortable seating and are a less formal alternative to tailored box or squab cushions. A specially cut foam shape (which can be ordered from good upholstery shops or specialist retailers) is simply covered with functional cotton gingham or ticking and pulled together with big stitches to create the padded look.

MATERIALS AND EQUIPMENT

thick cotton fabric
10 x 40 x 40cm (4 x 16 x 16in) fire-retardant foam block
dressmaker's pen
long straight upholsterer's needle
thick cotton yarn
ten 2.5cm (1in) self-cover buttons (optional)
sewing kit
sewing machine

CUTTING OUT

from the cotton fabric:
9 x 30cm (3½ x 12in) strip for the handle
four 13 x 43cm (5 x 17in) side strips
two 43cm (17in) squares for the top and bottom

NOTES

The measurements are based on a 40cm (16in) square: scale them up in proportion to make a larger cushion.

The seam allowance throughout is 1cm (½in).

I Press under a 1cm (½in) turning along all four edges of the handle strip, then press it in half lengthways with wrong sides together. Tack/baste the three open sides together and work a round of machine stitch on all four sides, 3mm (⅛in) from the edge.

2 Pin and tack/baste the handle in place along the centre of one of the side strips, looping it so that each end lies 10cm (4in) in from the short edge. Machine stitch several times across both ends of the handle.

3 With right sides together, pin and tack/baste the short edges of all four side strips together to make a square. Machine stitch each seam starting and ending 1cm (½in) from the corners. Press the seams open.

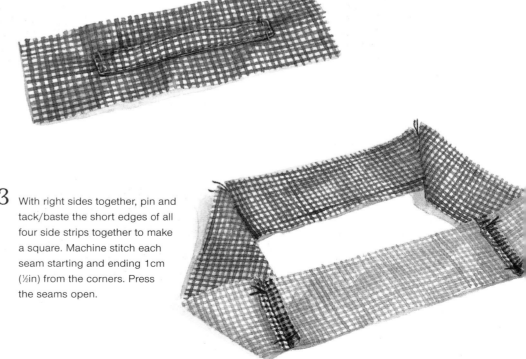

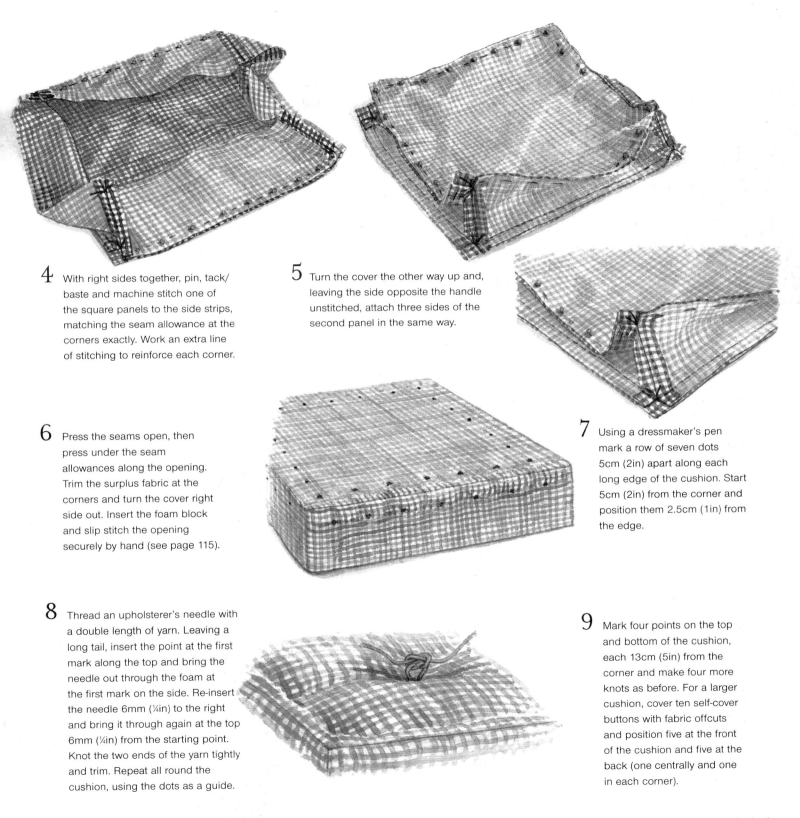

4   With right sides together, pin, tack/
    baste and machine stitch one of
    the square panels to the side strips,
    matching the seam allowance at the
    corners exactly. Work an extra line
    of stitching to reinforce each corner.

5   Turn the cover the other way up and,
    leaving the side opposite the handle
    unstitched, attach three sides of the
    second panel in the same way.

6   Press the seams open, then
    press under the seam
    allowances along the opening.
    Trim the surplus fabric at the
    corners and turn the cover right
    side out. Insert the foam block
    and slip stitch the opening
    securely by hand (see page 115).

7   Using a dressmaker's pen
    mark a row of seven dots
    5cm (2in) apart along each
    long edge of the cushion. Start
    5cm (2in) from the corner and
    position them 2.5cm (1in) from
    the edge.

8   Thread an upholsterer's needle with
    a double length of yarn. Leaving a
    long tail, insert the point at the first
    mark along the top and bring the
    needle out through the foam at
    the first mark on the side. Re-insert
    the needle 6mm (¼in) to the right
    and bring it through again at the top
    6mm (¼in) from the starting point.
    Knot the two ends of the yarn tightly
    and trim. Repeat all round the
    cushion, using the dots as a guide.

9   Mark four points on the top
    and bottom of the cushion,
    each 13cm (5in) from the
    corner and make four more
    knots as before. For a larger
    cushion, cover ten self-cover
    buttons with fabric offcuts
    and position five at the front
    of the cushion and five at the
    back (one centrally and one
    in each corner).

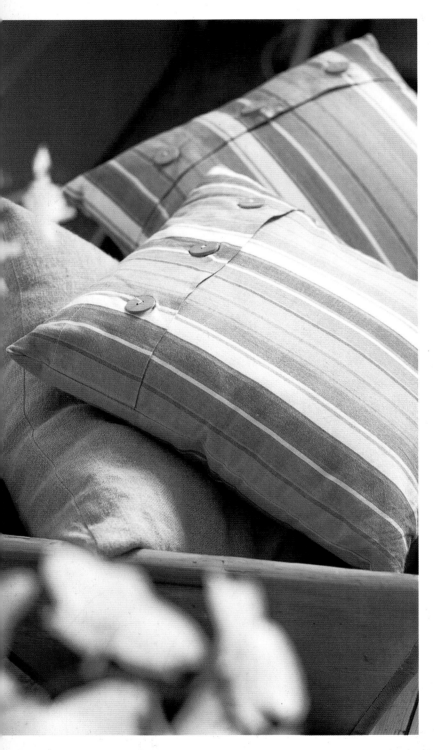

The word plaid is, in fact, derived from the Scottish Gaelic term for tartan, a fabric which has spawned an industry of its own. Many of the clan patterns – the dress kilts and the hunting variations – are an invention of the romantic early nineteenth century and come in bright reds and greens.

Tartan blankets are perfect if you have a baronial hunting lodge, but there are new interpretations with a more contemporary use of natural colours, such as mauve heathers, grass greens and pale sky blues, which are more adaptable for use in modern interiors.

Madras cottons from India and other more complex plaids are at home in living rooms but also fit well into conservatories and outdoor spaces. Checks and stripes appear together in many traditional interiors, particularly the muted Gustavian rooms of nineteenth-century Scandinavia and early American homes, where country weaves, plaids and ginghams jostled happily together. In a modern scheme, they work in the same way, complementing rather than matching their surroundings.

FAR LEFT If you are making cushion covers with an overlapped buttoned fastening like these, be sure to match up the stripes exactly.

LEFT French-style mattress ticking comes in almost every possible permutation of red, grey, beige and cream and the striped patterns vary greatly. Put them together, as on this coral sofa, and you can create a bold impact. See how they are made on page 52.

THIS PAGE Striped fabrics require little embellishment: the red piping is all that is needed to finish this cushion.

striped and piped cushion

These ticking cushions are a classic design from Jane Sacchi, which would be equally at home in a period-style room or a pared-down minimalist interior. Striped fronts contrast well with the plain linen backs, while the brightly coloured piping/cording, carefully chosen to coordinate with the stripes, gives definition to the square shape. The self-covered buttons provide the perfect finishing touch.

MATERIALS AND EQUIPMENT

striped fabric for front
plain fabric for back
coloured fabric for piping/cording
200m (80in) thick piping cord
two 6 x 50cm (2½ x 20in) strips of lightweight iron-on interfacing
dressmaker's fading pen
five 2.5cm (1in) self-cover buttons
50cm (20in) square cushion pad/form
matching sewing thread
sewing kit

CUTTING OUT

from striped fabric:
one 50cm (20in) square

from plain fabric:
one 50cm (20in) square
one 20 x 50cm (8 x 20in) strip

from the coloured fabric:
one 6 x 200cm (2½ x 80in) bias strip (see page 116)

I   Tack/baste the bias strip over the piping cord with right sides together. Tack/baste it in place on the right side of the front panel and join the ends as shown on page 116.

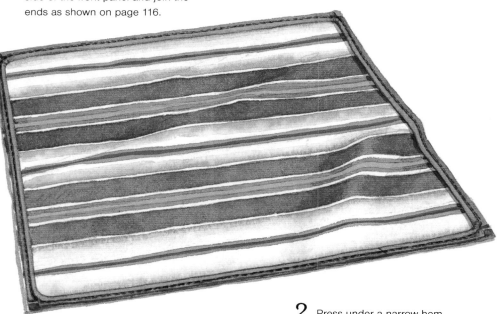

2   Press under a narrow hem along one side of the square back panel, then press under a 6cm (2½in) turning and unfold.

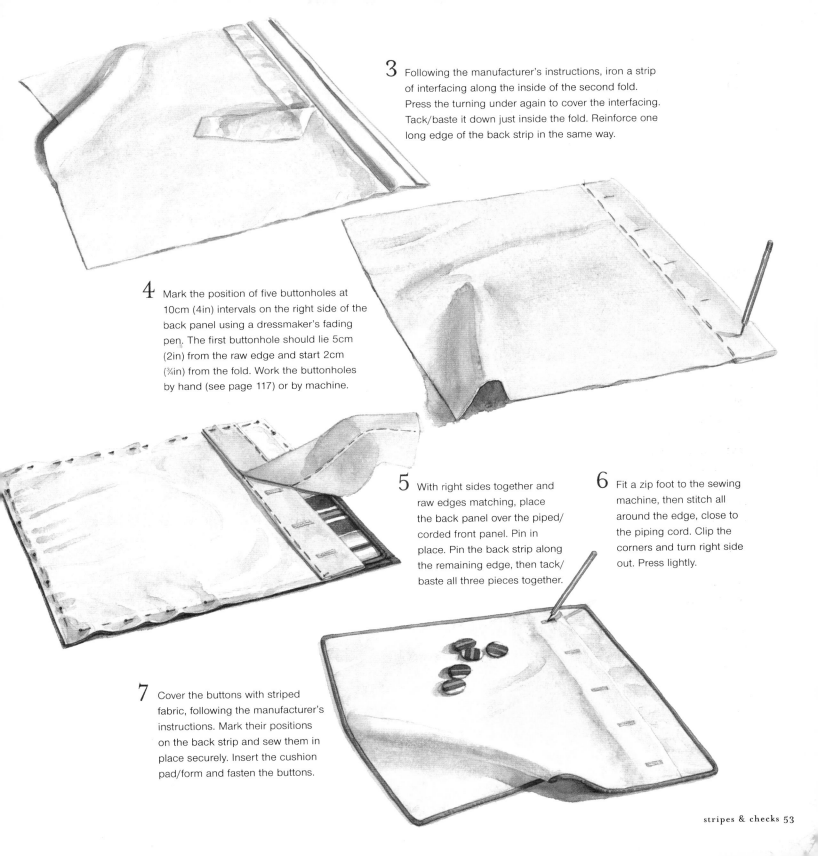

3 Following the manufacturer's instructions, iron a strip of interfacing along the inside of the second fold. Press the turning under again to cover the interfacing. Tack/baste it down just inside the fold. Reinforce one long edge of the back strip in the same way.

4 Mark the position of five buttonholes at 10cm (4in) intervals on the right side of the back panel using a dressmaker's fading pen. The first buttonhole should lie 5cm (2in) from the raw edge and start 2cm (¾in) from the fold. Work the buttonholes by hand (see page 117) or by machine.

5 With right sides together and raw edges matching, place the back panel over the piped/corded front panel. Pin in place. Pin the back strip along the remaining edge, then tack/baste all three pieces together.

6 Fit a zip foot to the sewing machine, then stitch all around the edge, close to the piping cord. Clip the corners and turn right side out. Press lightly.

7 Cover the buttons with striped fabric, following the manufacturer's instructions. Mark their positions on the back strip and sew them in place securely. Insert the cushion pad/form and fasten the buttons.

Flower prints and floral patterns have an undeniable and enduring appeal. Over the centuries the luscious shapes and colours of petals, buds and leaves have inspired a rich variety of textile designs, and contemporary furnishing fabrics continue to develop this perennial theme.

florals

BELOW The bands of flowers in this striped pink fabric echo the back struts of the faux-bamboo chair.

BOTTOM Quilts and cushions are natural partners and by selecting similar colour schemes, floral patterns from different eras can be combined effortlessly.

OPPOSITE Each of these six understated covers is made from a different but complementary fabric. Any piping/cording, fringing or other trim would detract from the beautiful designs.

LEFT Extravagantly scalloped edges and contrasting backing fabric add character to these two French cushions.

ABOVE A soft feather filling gives a congenial, worn-in look to two large antique print cushions.

Florals have always been a favourite with interior designers, and with good reason. Just as the flowers on display in our gardens vary depending on the time of year, floral fabrics come in their own seasonal ranges. So whatever mood you wish to create – contemporary, classic or shabby chic – you are guaranteed to find something to complement your scheme. Small-scale sprigged patterns of rosebuds, primroses and blossoms are always spring-like; ideal for boudoir-style bedrooms or light and airy living rooms. Prints starring big cabbagey roses or swathes of tropical blooms are reminiscent of high summer and look as good in the garden as they do inside. The deep green, red and russet fabrics that go so well with paisley prints are especially autumnal – colours that, with chocolate browns and pale frosty blues, will see you through to cold mid-winter and work well in warm, relaxed living spaces.

Historically, floral patterns have been anything from highly stylized to completely naturalistic. William Morris, whose furnishing fabrics have been in production since the 1870s, painted the roses that grew over the trellis in his own garden to achieve Pre-Raphaelite truth to nature. Other designers have looked to reference books: Elizabethan embroiderers copied the diagrams in their herbals and floral toiles were often based on the copperplate engravings that illustrated botanical works. Countless

anonymous artists drew up print designs for the workaday materials for eiderdowns, bedspreads, curtains and other modest domestic uses. With great, and often underestimated, skill they looked to the patterns in nature and combined flowers with paisleys, stripes, branches and leaves to create fabrics that have never lost their appeal and which are still imitated and reproduced today.

Fabric designs are often influenced by trends in the visual arts. As pop art exploded onto the scene in the 1960s and 1970s amid a riot of bold graphic colour, realistic florals moved into the shade in favour of over-scaled flowers, often stylized to the point of abstraction. Prints from this era, like those pioneered by the Finnish firm Marimekko, are once again being appreciated for their dynamism and energy.

The big new story in fabrics is laser printing technology, which offers us the ultimate realism. Dramatic close-up photographs of a single exotic bloom or the centre of an open flower can be transferred onto fabric, either as one-offs or for mass production. Made into a cushion cover, this could give as much impact to a plain sofa as an abstract picture can to an otherwise blank wall.

The way we perceive colour and pattern is inevitably influenced by what lies around it: a faded floral cushion would be a highlight within a neutral setting but is far less striking when surrounded by similar prints. When using florals, you need to be a little disciplined to keep the overall impression from becoming too overblown. It is usually best to keep to a narrow palette – sugar pinks, cloudy blues

OPPOSITE Floral prints look completely at home outdoors, picking up the natural colours of their surroundings. Here, dusky pink flowers on a beige background are enhanced by the dull silver-grey of a lavender bush.

ABOVE Vintage garden furniture is immensely stylish and practical for outdoor use, but it is not necessarily designed with comfort in mind. Thick padded and buttoned cushions, along with a matching quilted throw, make these metal-framed chairs a softer option.

RIGHT Two frilly-edged cushions lend a slightly frivolous air to a classic wrought-iron garden bench.

BELOW Embroidered with chain-stitch flowers in clear pink, gold, purple and red on a soft lilac background, this pashmina crosses the design boundary from fashion accessory to useful throw.

RIGHT Traditional flower prints will always look at home alongside each other, and seldom clash or jar. These old and new classic blooms are linked by a common colour theme.

OPPOSITE When you are selecting fabrics, remember that it is possible to create an eye-catching look simply by playing with scale. Try mixing large and small patterns in similar designs, whether they are checks, stripes or florals. This wall hanging has a graphic, meandering design of flowers and foliage, which is echoed on a much smaller scale by the cushion covers.

and pastel greens, or more saturated summer colours – and mix patterns on different scales. Add toning plains or stripes to give variety, rather than geometric prints. As an example, the classic English drawing room, typified by Colefax and Fowler in the mid-twentieth century, paired mostly green and pink prints with pale damask weaves for a romantic image that still looks fresh today.

When it comes to sourcing floral fabrics there are many avenues to explore. You can mix and mismatch designs from different eras, provided you keep to a common colour theme. So look for originals in good condition as well as new materials. High-street and contract suppliers have run-of-the-mill prints which can be mixed with new finds and remnants, but there are many specialists, including Cath Kidston and Cabbages and Roses, whose nostalgic prints have a charm all of their own. Be inspired by patchwork quilts and their unpretentious blending of fabrics, and balance plains and florals to create your own individual approach.

tie-on cushion cover

The informal covers on these giant floor cushions needed a simple approach: they had to be washable and hard-wearing, yet decorative. The slip covers on the large square cushions are fastened with narrow ties made from the main cover fabric – an unfussy fixture that can be undone easily when required.

MATERIALS AND EQUIPMENT

main fabric
63cm (25in) square cushion with plain cover (see page 119)
matching sewing thread
knitting needle
sewing kit
sewing machine

CUTTING OUT

for the ties:
four 5 x 30cm (2 x 12in) strips

for the front and back panels:
two 65cm (26in) squares

for the facings:
two 15 x 65cm (6 x 26in) strips

NOTE
The seam allowance throughout is 1cm (½in).

I To make the four ties, fold each strip of fabric in half lengthways, with right sides together. Pin and tack/baste together, then machine stitch along the long edge and one short edge. Clip the corners.

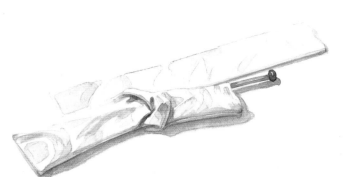

2 Turn each tie right side out. Ease the corners into shape using a knitting needle and press flat.

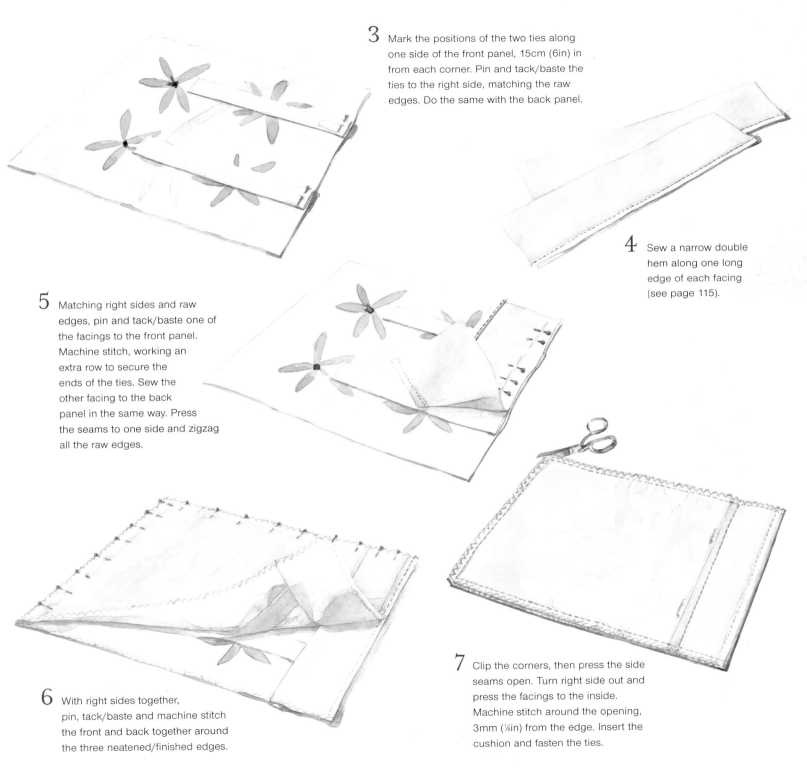

3 Mark the positions of the two ties along one side of the front panel, 15cm (6in) in from each corner. Pin and tack/baste the ties to the right side, matching the raw edges. Do the same with the back panel.

4 Sew a narrow double hem along one long edge of each facing (see page 115).

5 Matching right sides and raw edges, pin and tack/baste one of the facings to the front panel. Machine stitch, working an extra row to secure the ends of the ties. Sew the other facing to the back panel in the same way. Press the seams to one side and zigzag all the raw edges.

6 With right sides together, pin, tack/baste and machine stitch the front and back together around the three neatened/finished edges.

7 Clip the corners, then press the side seams open. Turn right side out and press the facings to the inside. Machine stitch around the opening, 3mm (⅛in) from the edge. Insert the cushion and fasten the ties.

florals 63

Embellishment — the antidote to minimalism —
is a reaction against a decade of understated
good taste and a wonderful way to bring a
touch of glamour into our lives. Embroidery
and decorative needlecrafts are once again
being recognized as intrinsically valuable
and now feature in the most stylish of homes.

patchwork & embellishments

OPPOSITE Patchwork on a very large scale makes an oversized throw for a long, low-backed sofa.

LEFT Suffolk Puff, or Yo-yo patchwork, is made from circles of fabric. Run a gathering thread around the perimeter of each circle, draw it up and fasten off. Gently flatten the resulting puffball. Stitch together in rows, then sew on to the edge of a coordinating cushion.

RIGHT The stylized white embroidery on this chambray pillowcase reflects the crisp cotton border. See how to make it on page 76.

BELOW RIGHT This glorious Victorian diamond patchwork throw is embellished with elaborate stitching.

BELOW LEFT The reflective satin fabrics and pearl buttons used on this cushion cover contrast with the soft sheen of the silk and velvet patches.

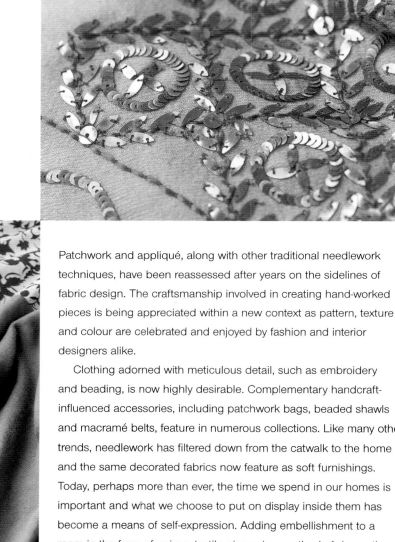

RIGHT Silver metallic embroidery worked on a background of pale ochre makes for a sophisticated combination of texture and colour.

BELOW A detail of the throw from the previous page shows the designer's skilful matching of seemingly diverse fabrics: four different prints and an embroidered shawl blend without jarring.

OPPOSITE The richly fringed, encrusted throw and coordinating cushion are offset by the plainer texture and pattern of the grey and cream cushion cover.

Patchwork and appliqué, along with other traditional needlework techniques, have been reassessed after years on the sidelines of fabric design. The craftsmanship involved in creating hand-worked pieces is being appreciated within a new context as pattern, texture and colour are celebrated and enjoyed by fashion and interior designers alike.

Clothing adorned with meticulous detail, such as embroidery and beading, is now highly desirable. Complementary handcraft-influenced accessories, including patchwork bags, beaded shawls and macramé belts, feature in numerous collections. Like many other trends, needlework has filtered down from the catwalk to the home and the same decorated fabrics now feature as soft furnishings. Today, perhaps more than ever, the time we spend in our homes is important and what we choose to put on display inside them has become a means of self-expression. Adding embellishment to a room in the form of unique textile pieces is a method of decorating that can be truly individual.

It may be wise, however, to err on the side of minimalism when introducing dense pattern and intense colour into the home. Too much ornamentation can prove difficult to live with on a daily basis and no longer suits a contemporary lifestyle – think of the cluttered nineteenth-century parlours, where a plethora of chenille table covers, tapestry cushions, beaded trinket boxes and doilies vied for space on every surface. Nevertheless, it is possible to create a more

OPPOSITE Large panels of printed fabric in rich floral and paisley patterns have been patched together with flower-sprigged pashminas for a sumptuous throw and two huge cushions that make this sofa the focal point of a relaxed living room.

LEFT A close-up of one of the cushions reveals the intricate stitch-work of the stylized border, chosen to complement the more graphic flower print of the main fabric.

modern sense of opulence and even a slight, but fashionable, air of decadence by incorporating just a limited number of these elements into your living space.

Decorative textiles work best in a relatively neutral setting where there are no other visual distractions and where they can be given the space to become the main focus of interest. A beautiful *objet d'art*, for example, has far more impact in isolation than it would amid a shelf of similar pieces. In the same way, a single, gorgeously decorated cushion can be seen to best advantage on a plain armchair or divan. Larger expanses of pattern and colour – a patchwork velvet throw, for example – look best on furniture covered with simple fabrics and ideally need plain walls and curtains behind

them. This doesn't mean, however, that the setting has to be bland or the upholstery limited to cream or white. Darker backgrounds give extra emphasis to rich colours and textures making them appear deeper and more sumptuous.

When you start looking for these special cushions and throws, you'll find that there is an enormous amount on offer in all price brackets, as well as a wealth of antique items and fabrics which can be converted into your own one-off items. Decorative fabrics are produced by almost every culture throughout the world and have been exported across the globe. Paisley shawls and hand-stitched pashminas make perfect throws, while lengths of sequined sari fabric can be used to cover beds or drape over a sofa. Colourful

Indian bedspreads always look good in the bedroom, but are equally impressive in living spaces. Hand-woven or resist-printed African fabrics are art pieces in themselves but adapt well to become lightweight throws or cushion covers, as do Indonesian batiks and Chinese silk embroidery.

Making your own cushions and throws is straightforward and enjoyable. When you are using beautiful fabrics the shapes need be only very basic and the practicalities section at the end of this book will guide you step by step through the sewing processes involved. Smaller pieces of velvet, brocade and satin, along with fragments of embroidery, can be pieced together to make patchwork. This doesn't necessarily have to be in conventional hexagon patterns or folk-art geometric blocks, but can be much more spontaneous and informal. Choose fabrics for their individuality, looking out for textures, prints and colours that complement each other, then stitch them together in simple squares and rectangles. The patchwork cushion and throw projects at the end of this chapter are good examples of how luxurious fabrics can be combined to great effect.

While patchwork is a method of creating an entirely new fabric by stitching together remnants of other textiles, appliqué is essentially an embellishment and a way of adding decoration to an existing piece of cloth. This can be as straightforward as tacking/basting lengths of velvet ribbon along the edge of a throw to make a border, or sewing felt flowers on to a woollen cushion by hand. Iron-on bonding web is a quick way of adding a motif to a cushion cover or throw, which can be neatened/finished by machine (follow the instructions described for the pyramid beanbags on page 106).

Intricate patterns and textures for cushion covers and throws can be achieved by combining appliqué and patchwork with decorative stitching or by simply embroidering motifs onto a plain background. All that is needed to create a design are a few different stitches and there are myriad threads, silks and wools in every colour imaginable.

LEFT An informal arrangement of padded red velvet, luxurious cushions and a beautiful embroidered Indian throw give this wooden settle a warm and inviting appearance.

ABOVE The stripes on this linen cover were created by hand-stitching narrow fabric strips onto the front panel using chain stitch and back stitch. A round of blue piping/cording frames the design.

THIS PAGE Cushion backs do not necessarily have to match the fronts – panels of complementary fabrics have been used on the reverse of these square cushions.

Embroidering a riot of stitches on to a vivid silk background or making a small panel of traditional 'crazy' patchwork are good ways to practice sewing and patchwork techniques.

For a really dazzling effect, your work can be embellished further with beads, sequins and buttons. Victorian embroiderers knew how to exploit the reflective qualities of glass and mother-of-pearl: they stitched pearls, beads and spangles. which gleamed in the gaslight, on to their needlepoint and Berlin wool work. In the same way, traditional Indian embroidery is often studded with small shisha mirrors to catch the bright sunlight of the sub-continent. Sparkly sequins and beads in every shape and shade can be bought by length, by weight or as ready-made motifs. For a quick result, be creative with an existing cushion by highlighting the fabric with tiny rocaille beads or large sequins. Sari shops and Indian fabric suppliers are a valuable source of shisha, sequins and a glittering array of braids and metallic ribbons. Haberdashers/notions counters, market stalls and upholstery suppliers also stock many diverse trimmings – the bobble edgings, fringing, satin cords and tassels known collectively as passementerie. These can all be stitched by hand around the edge of a cushion or throw as a finishing touch.

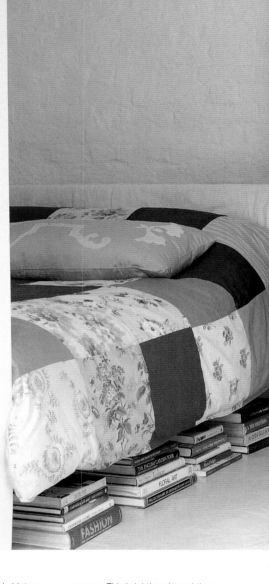

ABOVE Large squares of floral chintzes and plain satins were used to make this bedcover, which is specially shaped to fit around the bedposts. Similar patchwork could quickly be made using the swatches in fabric sample books.

LEFT The random selection and arrangement of the fabrics in this throw give it a spontaneous appeal. Instructions for making it can be found on page 78.

OPPOSITE This brightly coloured throw – a combination of patchwork and appliqué – looks enchanting in an outdoor candle-lit setting. Large squares of printed and woven metallic fabric are bordered with a framework of narrow stripes and joined together with wide bands of white cotton. These, in turn, are decorated with rows of appliquéd squares, set 'on point' in an intricate diamond pattern.

luxurious patchwork cushion

Despite its long heritage and historic tradition, a patchwork cushion doesn't have to be homespun or folksy. Textile artist Karen Spurgin works with opulent satins, brocades and velvets – the fabrics which she pieced together to make this refreshingly modern cushion. The contrasting textures and skilful choice of colours give it a sumptuous appearance, which is completed with a row of iridescent pearl buttons.

MATERIALS AND EQUIPMENT

a selection of silk and velvet remnants
55cm (22in) square matching backing fabric
matching sewing thread
ten 1cm (½in) pearl buttons
55cm (22in) square cushion pad/form
transparent nylon sewing thread
sewing kit

CUTTING OUT

a selection of 13cm (5in) wide pieces of different lengths for the patchwork strip
14 x 55cm (5½ x 22in) strip grey grosgrain
15 x 55cm (6 x 22in) strip red velvet
6 x 55cm (2½ x 22in) strip blue brocade
11 x 55cm (4½ x 22in) strip beige satin
9 x 55cm (3½ x 22in) strip blue satin

NOTES

These measurements are given as guidelines only, because the colours and proportions of your finished cover will vary depending on the fabrics used.

The seam allowance throughout is 1cm (½in).

I Lay the small pieces of fabric for the patchwork strip in a row, varying the colours and lengths. Pin, tack/baste and machine stitch with right sides together, until you have a strip that measures 55cm (22in) long. Press each seam lightly to one side, towards the thicker fabric, using a pressing cloth to protect the material.

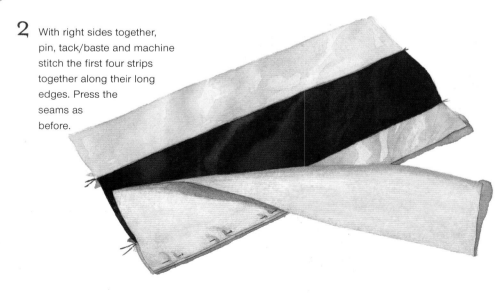

2 With right sides together, pin, tack/baste and machine stitch the first four strips together along their long edges. Press the seams as before.

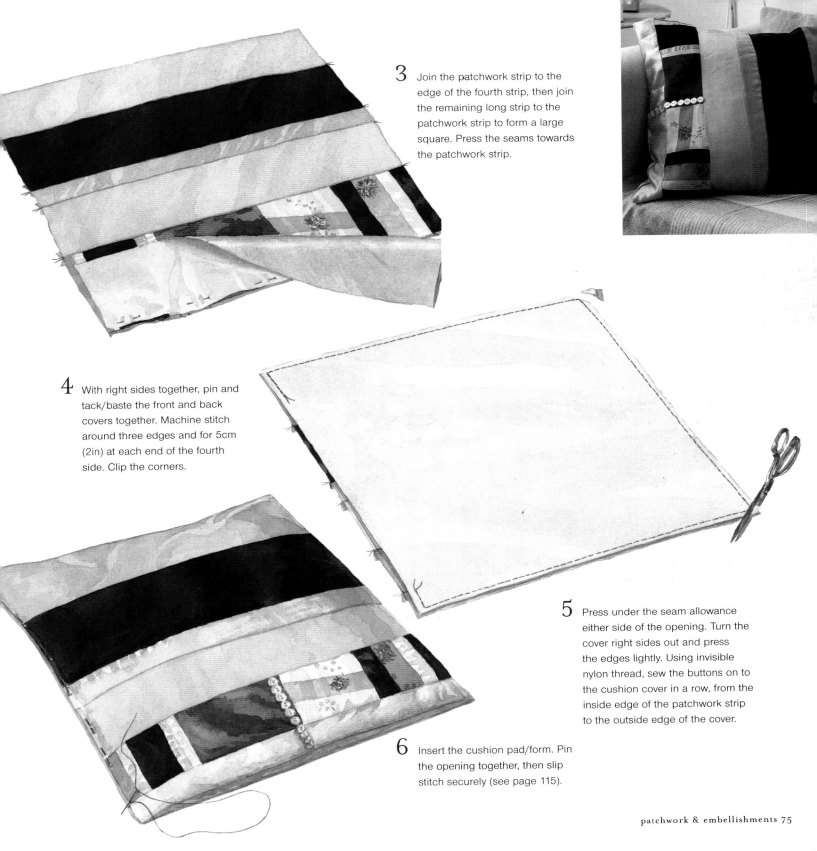

3 Join the patchwork strip to the edge of the fourth strip, then join the remaining long strip to the patchwork strip to form a large square. Press the seams towards the patchwork strip.

4 With right sides together, pin and tack/baste the front and back covers together. Machine stitch around three edges and for 5cm (2in) at each end of the fourth side. Clip the corners.

5 Press under the seam allowance either side of the opening. Turn the cover right sides out and press the edges lightly. Using invisible nylon thread, sew the buttons on to the cushion cover in a row, from the inside edge of the patchwork strip to the outside edge of the cover.

6 Insert the cushion pad/form. Pin the opening together, then slip stitch securely (see page 115).

oxford pillowcases with embroidery

My inspiration for the leaf pattern which decorates these pillowcases came from the stylized embroidery of the 1950s, when designers looked to natural forms for inspiration. The stitches used are basic and the motifs can be worked quickly, but, if you prefer a more minimal look, work a single leaf in one corner or omit the embroidery altogether.

I Cut a 20 x 69cm (8 x 27in) strip of tracing paper and fold it in half lengthways and widthways. Line up the creases with the broken lines across the motif (see page 122) and trace the outline with a sharp pencil. Turn the paper over and trace a reversed motif above and below the first, using the part motifs as a placement guide.

MATERIALS AND EQUIPMENT (FOR EACH PILLOW)

white cotton sheeting
tracing paper
69cm (27in) square cotton chambray
matching sewing thread
ruler
sharp pencil
dressmaker's carbon
three 20m (22 yard) skeins of thick (40) white coton à broder/mercerized cotton
embroidery needle
65cm (26in) square pillow
sewing kit
sewing machine

CUTTING OUT

from the cotton sheeting:
four 10 x 83cm (4 x 33in) border strips
one 25 x 83cm (10 x 33in) strip
one 65 x 83cm (26 x 33in) rectangle

NOTE
The seam allowance throughout is 1cm (½in).

2 Mark the centre of each edge of the chambray square. Matching the centre of the tracing paper to this point, pin the left edge to one side of the fabric. Trace the design on to the fabric using dressmaker's carbon. Do the same on the other three sides.

3 Embroider the motif using coton à broder/mercerized cotton. Use chain stitch for the leaf and top two spirals, three cross stitches for the leaf veins, stem stitch for the stalk and lower spirals and detached chain stitch for the three lines of dots. Fill in the stalk with satin stitch (see page 119 for how to work the stitches). Press from the wrong side when complete.

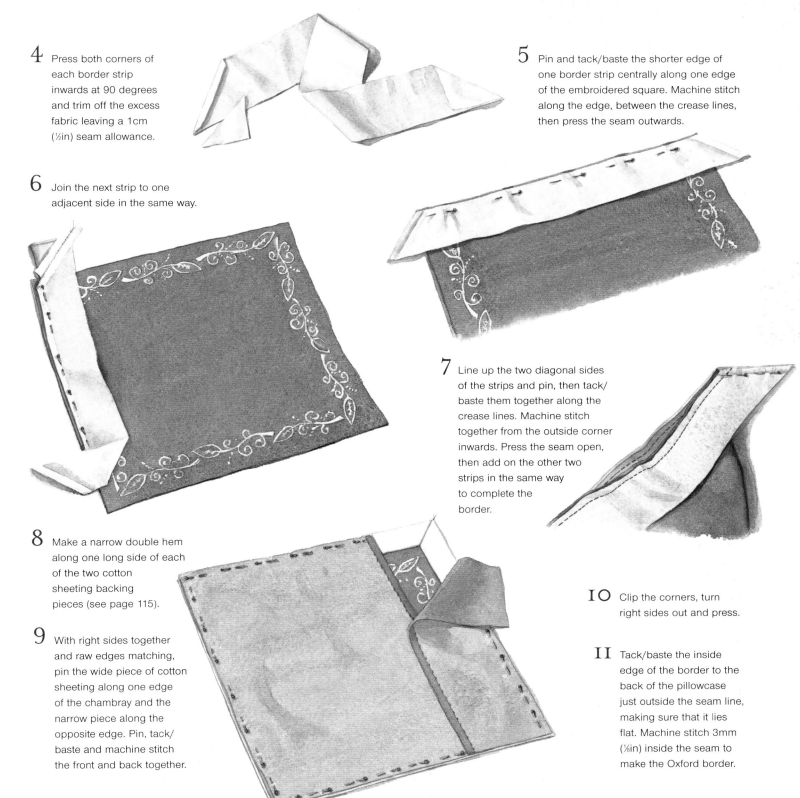

4 Press both corners of each border strip inwards at 90 degrees and trim off the excess fabric leaving a 1cm (½in) seam allowance.

5 Pin and tack/baste the shorter edge of one border strip centrally along one edge of the embroidered square. Machine stitch along the edge, between the crease lines, then press the seam outwards.

6 Join the next strip to one adjacent side in the same way.

7 Line up the two diagonal sides of the strips and pin, then tack/baste them together along the crease lines. Machine stitch together from the outside corner inwards. Press the seam open, then add on the other two strips in the same way to complete the border.

8 Make a narrow double hem along one long side of each of the two cotton sheeting backing pieces (see page 115).

9 With right sides together and raw edges matching, pin the wide piece of cotton sheeting along one edge of the chambray and the narrow piece along the opposite edge. Pin, tack/baste and machine stitch the front and back together.

10 Clip the corners, turn right sides out and press.

11 Tack/baste the inside edge of the border to the back of the pillowcase just outside the seam line, making sure that it lies flat. Machine stitch 3mm (⅛in) inside the seam to make the Oxford border.

giant patchwork throw

The charm of this traditional patchwork throw lies in the apparent randomness of the fabric arrangement and the wide variety of colours and textures used by designer Jeanie Blake. One quickly made diagonal block is repeated to create a pattern of concentric diamonds: to achieve a similar spontaneous look, try not to be too careful or contrived when selecting your materials and stitching the strips together.

MATERIALS AND EQUIPMENT

a selection of old and new fabrics
of similar weight
rotary cutter (optional)
quilter's ruler (optional)
cutting mat (optional)
30cm (12in) square of thick paper
to use as a template
tailor's chalk
175cm (69in) square of backing fabric
four 10 x 175cm (4 x 69in) wide strips
of plain fabric for the border
matching sewing thread
sewing kit
sewing machine

I   The patchwork blocks are pieced together roughly, then trimmed down to size using the paper template.

2   Sort out your fabrics, discarding any worn parts, then press them. Cut them into narrow strips of between 5–10cm (2–4in) wide. A rotary cutter and quilter's ruler which enable you to cut quickly and accurately will speed up this process, but are not essential.

3   Cut a 15cm (6in) length from one of the fabrics. Cut two shorter lengths from a different fabric, each with inward sloping ends, and join one to each side of the longer length with a 6mm (¼in) seam. Press the seams to one side. Continue adding further strips, each one shorter than the last, to make an approximate square. Check your work against the paper template as you go to make sure that it will be the right size.

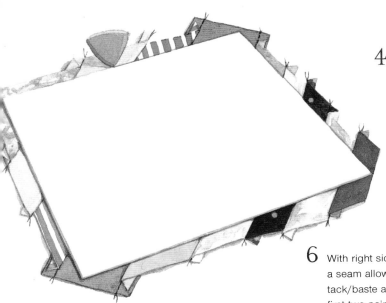

4 Put the template on top of the block of fabric and draw a line around it with tailor's chalk. Cut out around the line. Make another 35 blocks in the same way.

5 Lay the blocks out in six rows of six, alternating the direction of the fabric to form an overall diamond design. Take some time arranging them so that you get the best balance of pattern and colour within the design.

6 With right sides together and leaving a seam allowance of 1cm (½in), pin, tack/baste and machine stitch the first two pairs of blocks together. Press the seams to one side, then join the two pairs to make a large square. Sew the remaining blocks together in the same way to make eight more squares, then join the squares into three rows. Seam the rows together to complete.

7 Lay the backing fabric on the floor with the right side facing downwards. Place the patchwork centrally on top with the right side upwards and pin together around the outside edge, smoothing the layers from the centre to ensure they lie flat. Tack/baste together 1cm (½in) from the edge, then trim away the surplus backing fabric.

8 Press under 1cm (½in) along each side of the four strips of plain fabric, then press each one in half lengthways. Fold the first strip over one edge of the quilt and pin, then tack/baste in place. Stitch down by hand or machine and trim the binding in line with the corners.

9 Pin a folded strip to the next edge and trim 1cm (½in) from the end adjacent to the first strip. Press the overlap to the wrong side. Tack/baste, then stitch the strip down, and finish off the folded corner with slip stitch (see page 115). Repeat for the other two edges.

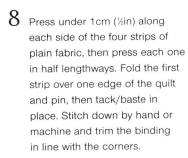

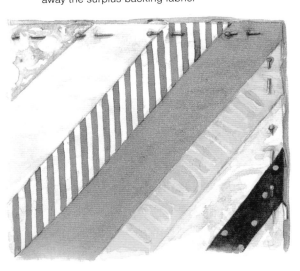

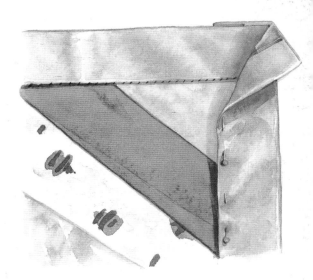

Despite the implied contradiction, modern vintage is an essentially contemporary style. It is a serendipitous approach to interiors, which seeks to reclaim the best of the past and combine it with the new to create a timelessness that goes beyond transient fashion.

salvage & vintage style

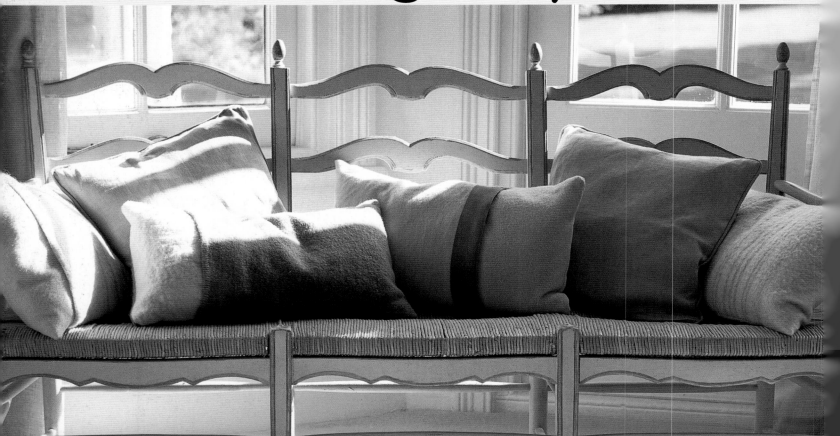

OPPOSITE Rectangular pillows double up as cushions when covered in thicker fabrics: here they serve to soften a long wooden bench.

LEFT Pillows trimmed with broderie anglaise, coupled with two rose print quilts evoke a sense of tranquillity. Instructions for making the pillowcases are given on page 86.

RIGHT Victorians displayed their favourite brooches by pinning them to small cushions then placing them on the dressing table. This glorious cushion gives a new twist to an old idea: see how it was made on page 90.

BELOW Three throws and an assortment of vintage-inspired print cushions give individual character to a plain sofa.

Vintage style is eclectic, easy to live with and very informal. The ethos that lies behind it is primarily about appreciating the unique qualities of old pieces that have survived the years and valuing them for their individuality, rather than simply purchasing expensive antiques in an attempt to imitate the past or reproduce a particular period. It is a look that works throughout the house, and can be adapted to bedrooms and bathrooms as well as living spaces.

Whether you visit specialist dealers at the top end of the market or prefer rummaging around at flea markets and boot sales, the search for vintage textiles and period accessories is immensely pleasurable and once you have started, the lure of the hunt is hard to resist. No two pieces are ever alike and no two people will utilize them in the same way, so whatever you discover and however you choose to display your finds, the look will be a very personal one.

Be relaxed in your approach. Mix furniture, ornaments and fabrics from different eras and diverse cultures – it doesn't matter if your rooms don't appear as coordinated as a show home. By creating contrasts within a room and pairing objects and textiles that might

not go together at a first impression, you can make your space as quirky and individual as you like. An old Anglepoise lamp, a fly-spotted Venetian mirror and a chrome-framed Corbusier armchair will look perfectly at home alongside an Indian wedding garland, embroidered cushions and the odd lacy doiley. The only criteria for choosing furniture and textiles is that you really like them and will enjoy living among them.

Antique fabrics have a comforting, worn-in feel and the exclusivity that comes from having outlasted decades of heavy use. Much of what survives dates from the frugal 'sides-to-middle era' of the nineteenth and twentieth centuries – a time when threadbare sheets were cut in half and the selvedges reseamed to prolong their useful life and outgrown jumpers were unravelled so that the wool could be reknitted. For many families, new materials were hard to come by and expensive, so thrift crafts like patchwork and rag-rug making were an economic necessity rather than a hobby. There is a wonderful legacy of domestic

OPPOSITE, BELOW LEFT Antique frocks often turn up at markets and textile fairs. Unworn parts of those beyond repair can be recycled to make glamorous cushions like these, which incorporate the original labels.

OPPOSITE, ABOVE RIGHT Remember that the tiniest scraps of fabric can be put to good use. A flower motif cut from a fragment of old material has been machine stitched onto this ticking cover.

THIS PAGE A collection of vintage fabrics will inevitably be diverse and too many patterns can look overwhelming. But when the palette is limited to just two colours, as here, the effect is calming.

craftwork to be explored, which, up until now, has been greatly undervalued. It is the end result of generations of skilful women spending many hours at home crocheting fine lace edgings, stitching together fragments of precious fabrics and embroidering napkins or tablecloths to adorn their surroundings. Such textiles can now be given a renewed life within a fresh context. You can continue this tradition by recycling your old denim jeans, striped shirts and treasured baby clothes to make your own heirlooms.

All old fabrics feel special but antique bed linen in particular has an appealing softness that can only be acquired by years of careful laundering and pressing. Monogrammed sheets and lace-trimmed pillowcases made from fine Egyptian cotton or hand-woven linen, which are still in good condition, are much sought after for these special qualities and can be costly – although they are rarely as expensive as their brand new equivalents.

OPPOSITE These Oxford pillowcases are contemporary reworkings of 1950s-style floral and spotty prints. Combined with a cherry red blanket and paisley eiderdown they look fresh, crisp and, above all, inviting.

ABOVE Monochrome toile de jouy flower and foliage prints – like those used for these classic red and white cushions – were the height of fashion in the 1770s and have retained their popularity for well over two centuries.

RIGHT A crisp linen pillowcase with a deep Oxford border is set off by a single detail: a vintage dress label in flowing script.

broderie anglaise pillowcases

The combination of cotton lace and crisp white sheeting gives a vintage look to this matching pair of pillowcases. I chose a wide broderie anglaise/eyelet border with a coordinating narrower insert to make the deep cuffs which overhang the side of the pillow. If you prefer, you could replace the cotton lace with strips cut from an openwork or embroidered fabric and simply seam them together.

MATERIALS AND EQUIPMENT

5cm (2in) wide cotton lace
20cm (8in) wide cotton lace
white cotton sheeting
white sewing thread
embroidery scissors or
curved nail scissors
two 50 x 75cm (20 x 30in) pillows
sewing kit
sewing machine

CUTTING OUT (FOR EACH PILLOWCASE)

from the sheeting:
one 1m x 58cm (39 x 23in)
rectangle
one 1m x 6cm (39 x 2½in) strip

from the lace:
1m (39in) narrow lace
1m (39in) wide lace

I Pin the narrow lace along the edge of the strip of sheeting, overlapping the lace on the right side of the sheeting by 2cm (¾in). Tack/baste securely in place, using small stitches so that it will not slip when machine stitched down.

2 Set the sewing machine to a 3mm (⅛in) closely-spaced zigzag and fit the satin stitch foot, if you have one. Machine stitch over the edge of the lace, following the outline as closely as possible.

3 Attach the wide lace to the other side of the sheeting strip following the same method. Sew the other side of the narrow lace to one long edge of the rectangle of cotton sheeting in the same way.

4 Using a pair of short-bladed embroidery scissors or curved nail scissors, carefully trim away the excess cotton fabric from the wrong side, cutting as close to the stitches as possible. Press the lace and fabric.

5 With right sides together, fold the pillowcase in half so that the lace forms a cuff, then pin and tack/baste the bottom and side edges together.

6 Machine stitch 1cm (½in) from the edge. Trim the seam allowance to 6mm (¼in) and neaten/finish with a wide zigzag or overlock stitch. Turn right side out and press.

A lot of the bed linen you will find comes from Europe and the pillowcases, therefore, tend to be mainly square or bolster-shaped. They are characterized by linen button fastenings and are often decorated with the original owners' initials, inset panels of crochet lace and touching embroidered mottoes.

To recreate the look, you can customize plain linen with your own embroidered monograms and old or new crochet edgings. Or recycle the best parts of damaged sheets to make cushion covers or pillowcases. The instructions for a basic 'housewife' slip are given on page 118 and the step-by-step project on page 86 shows you how to make an open-ended cover with a broderie anglaise/eyelet edging. Unworn cotton sheets can be made into duvet covers or cut down for cots and children's beds, while heavier linen will make lightweight throws (see the project on page 18).

The vogue for shabby chic has revived interest in all that is faded and vintage, and the demand for authentic soft furnishings, quilts and handicrafts is beginning to outstrip supply. There are still lots of quilts, shawls and cushions about, but if you cannot find originals to suit your purpose, or if you prefer to make your own covers and throws, there are plenty of convincing vintage-style reproductions around.

If you find a strongly patterned material that you like but you prefer a more muted look, there are two old decorator's tips that you can borrow. First, wash the fabric to remove any dressings then soak it in cold tea to tone down the colours. Or, bearing in mind that a bright print will always be paler on the reverse, use the back of the material as the right side when making up your project.

Designer Cath Kidston is the doyenne of nostalgia. Along with a wonderful and often light-hearted selection of period pieces, she sells a range of floral, paisley and pictorial fabrics, which are influenced by the past, but look unmistakably modern. Laura Ashley prints have been with us since the sixties, while Cabbages and Roses and The Laundry produce inspiring ranges of fabrics and accessories.

OPPOSITE, LEFT A family snapshot has been printed onto fine fabric and machine stitched onto a plain background. The texture is created by snipping between the lines of stitching.

OPPOSITE, RIGHT Rings of tiny pearl beads have been sewn onto this recycled denim cushion. This embroidered detailing is repeated on the antique flags.

THIS PAGE Painting the walls, floor and furniture in shades of white gives cohesion and provides a blank canvas against which the inventive textile art can be properly appreciated.

jewelled cushion

Designer Karen Nichol is an inveterate collector with an expert's eye for the quirky and the unusual. Her studio is a treasure trove, the accumulation of long hours spent scouring markets and secondhand sales for vintage costume jewellery, silk flowers, buttons, beads and ribbons, all of which influence or are incorporated into her work. This sparkling cushion is a wonderful showcase for a collection of diamanté/rhinestone buckles, brooches and dress clips.

MATERIALS AND EQUIPMENT

two 50cm (20in) squares of fine soft suede or suede-look fabric
matching sewing thread
45cm (18in) square cushion pad/form
19 brooches and buckles
low-tack masking tape
small pliers
sewing kit

I Clean all the pieces of jewellery with a soft cloth and check that all the paste jewels are fixed. Use a pair of small pliers to secure the settings as necessary.

2 Choose one of the larger items to be the centre of the arrangement and place this in the middle of one suede square. Lay seven small buckles in a circle around it.

3 Arrange the remaining pieces around the edge in a circle. Leave a margin of at least 5cm (2in) around the outside. The final look will depend on the size and shape of your own jewellery.

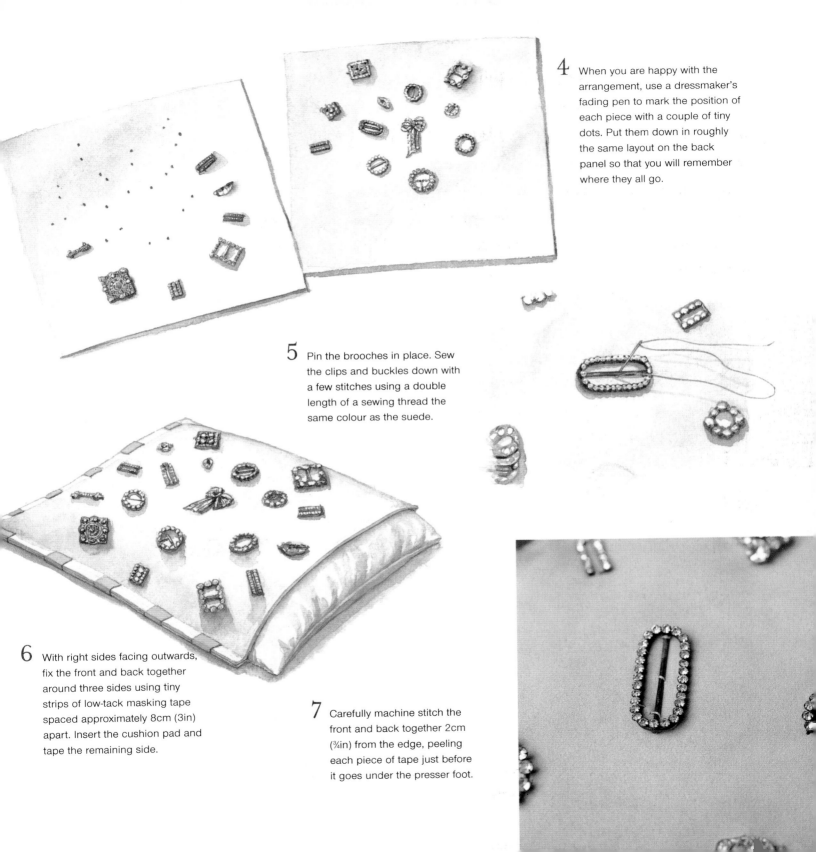

4 When you are happy with the arrangement, use a dressmaker's fading pen to mark the position of each piece with a couple of tiny dots. Put them down in roughly the same layout on the back panel so that you will remember where they all go.

5 Pin the brooches in place. Sew the clips and buckles down with a few stitches using a double length of a sewing thread the same colour as the suede.

6 With right sides facing outwards, fix the front and back together around three sides using tiny strips of low-tack masking tape spaced approximately 8cm (3in) apart. Insert the cushion pad and tape the remaining side.

7 Carefully machine stitch the front and back together 2cm (¾in) from the edge, peeling each piece of tape just before it goes under the presser foot.

Modern retro — the style of the
mid-twentieth century — marked a
significant milestone in domestic and
interior design. It was an era when
new furniture, textiles and accessories
were genuinely forward looking and
exciting, and surviving pieces are now
recognized as design classics.

retro & geometric

OPPOSITE A mixture of strong geometric prints – like this set of graphic cushion covers – is always going to be striking. Arranged along a low sofa, these cushions have a seventies look which is undeniably young and urban.

LEFT A neatly folded geometric throw in seventies' brown, black and white covers a tubular-legged chair. It is topped by an embroidered cushion cover in a complementary modernist pattern.

RIGHT Used in moderation, strong pattern will provide focus within a room. These fresh lime green and white pillowcases are balanced by a plain white sheet and quilted bedcover.

BELOW The accessories in this metropolitan living space are few, but carefully selected. The two cushions provide an understated counterpoint to the plain lines of the sofa and table.

OPPOSITE Strong geometric prints should not be used exclusively in minimalist room schemes. Here a cushion adorned with two dynamic spirals is shown to advantage against a seductively tactile faux fur throw and amid a selection of vintage accessories.

BELOW As with so many design styles, these retro cushions work especially well on a plain sofa. The geometric structure of the built-in shelving and the brightly coloured spines of the books are echoed by the three curvilinear 1970s-influenced designs.

The first years of the 1950s in Britain were dubbed the 'New Elizabethan age' as, after a decade of wartime austerity, people were looking optimistically to the future. A new generation of designers was emerging and fashionable homes began to acquire a radically modern and different style – the domestic counterpart of Dior's New Look. Alongside innovative forms in furniture by designers such as Eames, Jacobson and Race, abstract patterns began to appear on household accessories, ceramics, textiles, wallpaper and novel surfaces like formica. These imaginary designs were a striking fusion of bold shapes and vivid colours which appear as fresh today as they did then.

Textile designers in particular were producing vibrant work and encompassing new developments in technology. They drew a degree of inspiration from the geometric forms of Art Deco and the art of the Bauhaus that had developed in the 1930s, but, unusually, they made no reference to the more distant past. Influences ranged from paintings by Klee, Picasso and Paolozzi, to scientific images such as molecular and crystal structures. Conventional flower and foliage patterns were nowhere to be seen.

The most famous furnishing fabric was Lucienne Day's Calyx which was first exhibited at the Festival of Britain in 1951. By the following year it was the best selling textile on the American market. Day defined the pattern as having a 'sense of growth, but not floral': it was organic and natural but not representational. Variations on the themes of spindly lines, blocks of colour and geometric shapes all printed in avant-garde colour schemes – including cherry reds, lime yellows, mustards and chartreuse – dominated the market, but more graphic prints, often verging on the kitsch, were equally popular.

Successive generations have always looked back at their parents' era with a slight derision as they move on to new and better things, but fashion trends progress in ever-decreasing circles. The transition from laughable to cult takes about 30 years, and 1970s geometric prints, crocheted afghans and original Habitat furniture are once again in vogue. The huge scale of furnishing fabric designs from this period makes them ideally suited to large loft spaces where they can finally take centre stage, rather than appearing somewhat

OPPOSITE The polka was a Bohemian folk dance which spread across Europe and America in the 1840s. Its namesake – the familiar all-over pattern made up of regularly spaced coloured circles on a contrasting background – has been enduringly fashionable since that time.

ABOVE AND RIGHT The free, swirling pattern of this woollen throw provides the perfect foil for the geometric spots of the cushion cover. United by a common colour scheme of egg-yolk yellow and white, the two fabrics are close cousins.

OPPOSITE Mies van der Rohe's Barcelona chair is a design classic. It was first exhibited in 1929 and is still in production. This version is upholstered in buttoned white leather which sets off two retro-style cushions perfectly.

LEFT AND BELOW The solid borders – in colours picked out from the rosebud prints – add definition to the shape of these two personalized cushions. See how to make them on page 100.

overpowering in a smaller room. Combined with the best from contemporary designers they can look modernistic and as inventive as the styles of the fifties and sixties.

Seventies' fabrics are characterized by a bold use of sometimes brash pattern and unexpected colour schemes, such as chocolate browns, tangerines, turquoise, purples and lemons. There are a lot of original fabrics still about, but textile designers are continuing to work along the same themes producing strongly patterned fabrics, which complement sleek minimalism or enhance modern and post-modern furniture. If you want to introduce a retro touch to a living room, a few cushions and a throw made from a seventies-inspired geometric will add a splash of colour without giving a full period look.

If you grew up in the seventies you will remember, without nostalgia, the sheets and pillowcases of the time. Fortunately, yellow and orange brushed nylon has not undergone a similar revival. However, you can now find wonderful contemporary geometric bed linen designs that retain the spirit of the seventies' bedroom without the discomfort.

old photograph

plain white cotton fabric

plain coloured fabric (to coordinate
with the patterned fabric)

matching sewing thread

patterned fabric

two matching buttons (optional)

35 x 45cm (14 x 18in) cushion pad/form

sewing kit

sewing machine

CUTTING OUT

from plain coloured fabric:

for the inner border

two 5 x 15cm (2 x 6in) strips

two 5 x 30cm (2 x 12in) strips

for the outer border

two 5 x 35cm (2 x 14in) strips

two 5 x 50cm (2 x 20in) strips

for the back

one 6 x 40cm (2½ x 16in) strip

from patterned fabric:

for the main border

two 10 x 20cm (4 x 8in) strips

two 10 x 45cm (4 x 18in) strips

for the back

two 30 x 40cm (12 x 16in) rectangles

NOTES

The above measurements are for a 15 x 25cm
(6 x 10in) picture and a 35 x 45cm (14 x 18in)
rectangular cushion: adapt them as necessary
to fit the shape and proportions of your own
photograph and pad/form.

The seam allowance throughout is 1cm (½in).

transfer print cushion Instead of keeping

your old family photographs tucked away in albums you can
transfer the images onto fabric and make them into cushions
to keep for yourself or to give as nostalgic presents. These
covers feature my own favourite black-and-white snapshots and,
to complete the vintage look, I made the borders from sixties'
dressmaking material. Most high-street printers can copy
photographs on to iron-on transfer paper, which is available from
stationers if you want to print digital images from a computer.

I   Transfer your image on to the
white cotton fabric and trim it
down to 15 x 25cm (6 x 10in).

2   With right sides together, pin, tack/
baste and machine stitch the short
plain-coloured inner border strips to the
shorter sides of the picture. Carefully press
the seams outwards using a pressing cloth so
that the iron doesn't come into contact with the
transferred image. Attach the two long inner borders
to the long edges of the picture in the same way.

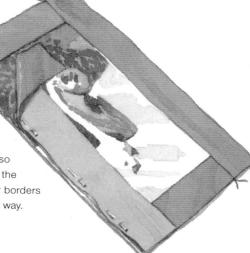

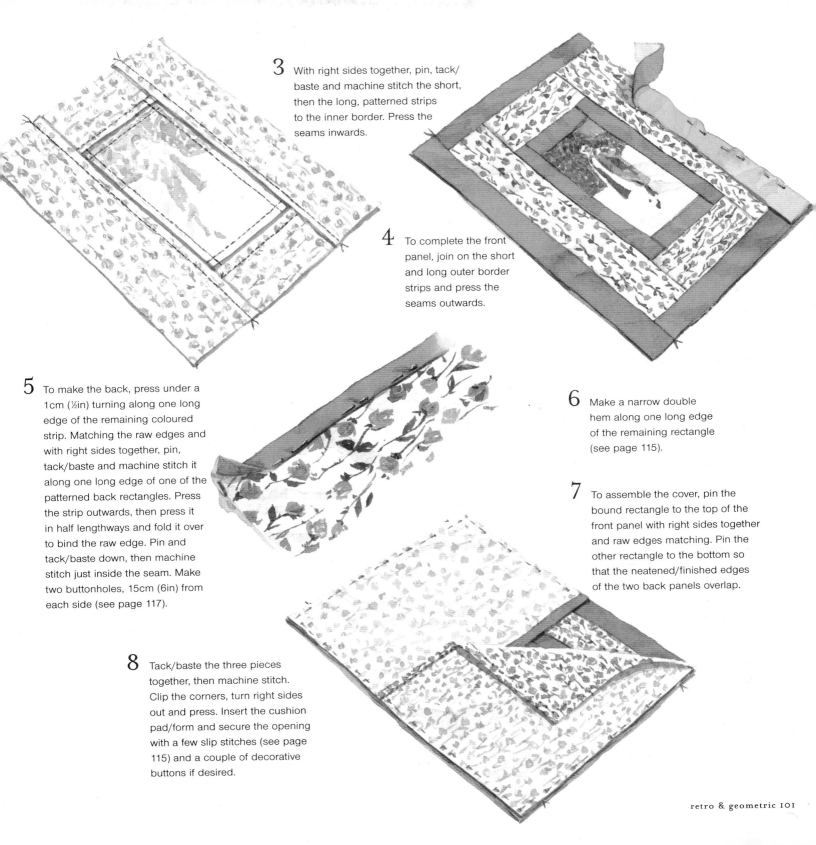

3 With right sides together, pin, tack/baste and machine stitch the short, then the long, patterned strips to the inner border. Press the seams inwards.

4 To complete the front panel, join on the short and long outer border strips and press the seams outwards.

5 To make the back, press under a 1cm (½in) turning along one long edge of the remaining coloured strip. Matching the raw edges and with right sides together, pin, tack/baste and machine stitch it along one long edge of one of the patterned back rectangles. Press the strip outwards, then press it in half lengthways and fold it over to bind the raw edge. Pin and tack/baste down, then machine stitch just inside the seam. Make two buttonholes, 15cm (6in) from each side (see page 117).

6 Make a narrow double hem along one long edge of the remaining rectangle (see page 115).

7 To assemble the cover, pin the bound rectangle to the top of the front panel with right sides together and raw edges matching. Pin the other rectangle to the bottom so that the neatened/finished edges of the two back panels overlap.

8 Tack/baste the three pieces together, then machine stitch. Clip the corners, turn right sides out and press. Insert the cushion pad/form and secure the opening with a few slip stitches (see page 115) and a couple of decorative buttons if desired.

Far more than simply a space to store clothes and toys or to sleep in at the end of the day, a child's bedroom should be a haven for a personal world of make-believe. Transform it into a special place for play, fantasy and relaxation, where the young imagination can run riot and dreams can unfold.

ideas for children

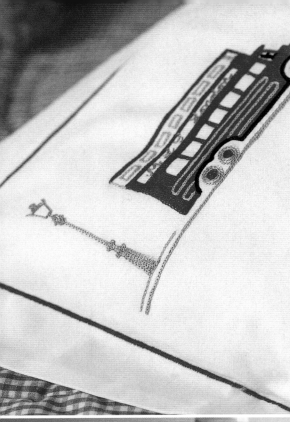

OPPOSITE Two stacks of small pillows soften a traditional iron bedstead during the day and make a comforting nest at bedtime.

LEFT Maybe it's something to do with the colour, but all children seem to adore London buses.

RIGHT These felt strawberries, speckled with hand-embroidered seeds, are tactile and tempting.

BELOW RIGHT A white room does not have to be austere: three plump cushions, a flowery eiderdown and a heart-sprinkled duvet give warmth to this attic space.

BELOW LEFT The children's characters we grew up with have become classics. This Babar cushion and soft toy appeal to all generations.

THIS PAGE Two matching pairs of ticking and gingham cushions, a peg rail and a small-scale sleigh bed are timeless accessories for a light and airy bedroom. Pattern has been kept to a minimum – the only motif being a repeated heart shape – and the colour scheme is limited to classic red, blue and white. Only the charming crocheted toys divulge the young age of the inhabitant of this bedroom.

OPPOSITE, BELOW A bear in a striped matelot jumper lies on an embroidered seaside cushion. Sailing boats have long been a favourite motif for children's rooms and there are plenty of accessories that fit in with a nautical theme.

OPPOSITE, TOP RIGHT These squidgy pyramid-shaped beanbags can be sat on, slept on or climbed over. See page 106 for instructions on how to make them.

When it comes to planning and decorating bedrooms or play areas for children – whatever their age – take inspiration from the memories of your own youth. Revisit your childhood to try to recapture something of the fun and exuberance of your earliest years. Can you remember when there seemed to be no rules and no preconceptions about anything, least of all interior design?

Small children are naturally attracted to bright colours, strong patterns and familiar images, whatever form they take. So try to incorporate all these elements into their surroundings to give them a lively and spontaneous flavour.

Bear in mind that a room scheme should develop with the child and accommodate his or her changing tastes and needs – the

bedroom of a boisterous toddler serves a very different purpose to a teenager's private and fiercely-guarded hideaway. With a little forethought, however, you can plan a space that is both stylish and adaptable and one that your children can grow up with happily.

If you are starting a room from scratch and furnishing a nursery for a new baby, it may be tempting to go for the full-on coordinated look available from high-street stores. Changing tables, cots and dressers, complete with matching rugs, curtains and wallpaper may be the ideal solution for the first few years, but they are expensive, soon outgrown and, when the design choices have already been made for you, they provide little scope for individuality. It is far better (and more economical in the long run) to start off with a few good pieces of basic furniture, plain walls and ceiling, and a simple floor covering. You can then introduce blocks of colour and pattern by means of the soft furnishings, bedding and accessories. These can easily be changed and updated, and the furniture can be repainted when a new look is demanded.

pyramid beanbags
An endearing gingham cat and rabbit smile out from these bright pyramid floor cushions. The fleece covers are quick to remove and washable, while the inner pads/forms, filled with polystyrene/styrofoam beads, are squashy and warm. They are lightweight enough for children to drag easily around the house in search of their favourite sitting place.

MATERIALS AND EQUIPMENT

60 x 120cm (24 x 48in) rectangle of fire-resistant interlining

bag of fire-resistant polystyrene/ styrofoam beads

sharp pencil

iron-on bonding web

25cm (10in) square of cotton gingham

offcut of contrasting gingham

60 x 120cm (24 x 48in) rectangle of knitted fleece fabric

offcut of contrasting fleece or felt

chalk pencil

sewing thread (to match gingham)

sewing thread (to match fleece)

black sewing thread

two buttons for the eyes

50cm (20in) nylon zip

sewing kit

sewing machine

WARNING: Always use a pressing cloth when ironing fleece or it will melt.

I   Mark the centre of both long edges of the interlining with a pin. Pin, tack/baste and machine stitch the two short edges together leaving a 1cm (½in) allowance and press the seam open.

2   Match the centre point of the bottom edge to the bottom of the seam and pin the two sides together to make a bag. Tack/ baste, then machine stitch 1cm (½in) from the edge.

3   Pin the top edge together in the opposite direction, starting at the seam and leaving a 20cm (8in) gap at the end for filling. Tack/ baste and machine stitch leaving a 1cm (½in) allowance, then turn the lining right side out. Press under the seam allowance along the gap.

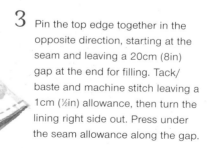

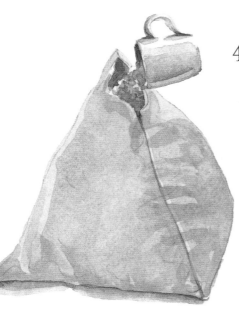

4 Using a mug as a scoop, three-quarters fill the lining with polystyrene/styrofoam beads, leaving enough empty space for it to squash down. Pin and tack/baste the opening to close, then machine stitch across the seam.

5 Enlarge the two animal templates on page 123 as directed. Using a pencil, trace the main outline, the inside ears, collar and nose on to the paper side of the bonding web. Cut them out leaving a narrow margin around each shape.

6 Following the manufacturer's instructions, iron the face on to the large piece of gingham, the ears on to the gingham offcut, the collar on to the fleece offcut and the nose on to a scrap of the main fleece. Cut out each piece around the outline.

7 Fix the face centrally to the fleece rectangle, then add the ears, nose and collar. Draw in the mouth using a chalk pencil.

8 Thread the sewing machine with the contrasting thread and satin stitch around the face and collar to conceal the raw edges. Sew around the nose and ears in the main colour and add the mouth in black. Finish off by sewing on the two buttons for the eyes.

9 Mark the centre of the two long edges of the fleece rectangle with a pin. With right sides of the fleece together, pin and tack/baste the short edges together leaving a 2cm (¾in) allowance. Machine stitch a 4cm (1¾in) seam at each end, then press the seam open. Insert the zip (see page 118).

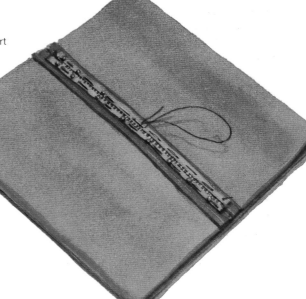

10 Undo the zip. Join the top and bottom of the cover as for the interlining (see Steps 2–3). Turn right side out, insert the beanbag and close the zip.

Young children's rooms are not really the place for subtle colours. You only have to look at their boxed games, dolls, fluffy toys and picture books to be confronted with an onslaught of bright primaries. So look to crisp greens, vivid reds and clear blues as a starting point for the soft furnishings. A jumbled mix of stripes, checks and cheerful ginghams always work well together and would look good in either a boy's or girl's room.

If you prefer to incorporate some pattern, there are some great retro-style prints about, featuring cowboy or seaside themes. However, special children's fabrics, depicting beloved cartoon characters, super heroes or pop idols, are bound to be their favourites and, if you don't want to be accused of style fascism, there may be times when you have to compromise with the provision of the odd cushion cover. But if you start out with a simple, classic theme of which your offspring approves – nautical stripes, spots, colourful fruit and flowers or Shaker-inspired folk art – you can share your enthusiasm and build on it together by adding curtains, stacks of cushions, throws and new bed linen. Whatever fabrics you choose should be hard-wearing and easy to care for, as they are bound to get well used, covered in sticky fingerprints and scribbled upon.

Children – and their carers – spend a lot of time playing, sitting and simply rolling about on the floor, so a few large, robust cushions or beanbags will make life a bit more comfortable. You may also find it useful to have a couple of spare travel rugs or large quilts in the playroom or bedroom. They will provide extra bedding, but will also double up as soft play mats, cover an armchair or sofa to protect the upholstery or stand in as a magic flying carpet when necessary.

LEFT Setting the scene for a Wild West adventure, an authentic-looking tepee sits in the corner of a toy-filled bedroom. Inside, to make playtime more comfortable, are a folded quilt, printed with a vintage-style design of wagons and cowboys, and two rather more grown-up stripy cushions.

ABOVE LEFT A pattern of cactuses and lasso-toting cowboys decorates this deceptively sophisticated children's cushion. A round of inset ric-rac makes a light-hearted border.

OPPOSITE, ABOVE LEFT Traditional folklore patterns, like the small blue bird perched on this fanciful tree, will always appeal to children, without being childish or twee.

OPPOSITE, ABOVE RIGHT The colours used here for the embroidery are repeated in the striped fabric that backs the pillow.

OPPOSITE, BELOW This traditional quilt is given an up-to-date twist with a row of appliqué felt cars: instructions for making it are on page 110.

gingham quilt

Cot quilts are popular presents for new babies who can lie on them when very small or be wrapped up in them for outings. As the child grows, the quilt takes on a new role as a bedcover or play mat. This undeniably contemporary gingham quilt continues a long-established custom.

MATERIALS AND EQUIPMENT

one 120 x 135cm (48 x 54in) rectangle of polyester wadding/ synthetic batting

two 110 x 125cm (43 x 50in) rectangles of red gingham

pair of compasses

thick tracing paper

sharp pencil

blue chalk dressmaker's pencil

long ruler

quilting thread or walking foot attachment for sewing machine

turquoise felt

scraps of blue, green and yellow gingham

skein of red stranded embroidery cotton

six 2.5cm (1in) self-cover buttons

matching sewing thread

I Lay the wadding/batting flat, place the two pieces of gingham, right sides together, centrally on top of it and smooth them out. Pin, then tack/baste together around all four edges.

2 Machine stitch 1cm (½in) from the edge, leaving a 50cm (20in) gap in the centre of one edge. Pin and tack/baste under the seam allowance along either side of the gap. Trim the surplus wadding/ batting and clip the corners.

3 Turn right side out through the gap so the wadding/ batting is sandwiched between the two pieces of gingham. Close the gap by hand with small slip stitches (see page 115) and press the seams lightly.

Use the compasses to make two quarter circle templates from thick tracing paper, with diameters of 17 and 19cm (7 and 7½in). Enlarge the two heart templates on page 122 as directed.

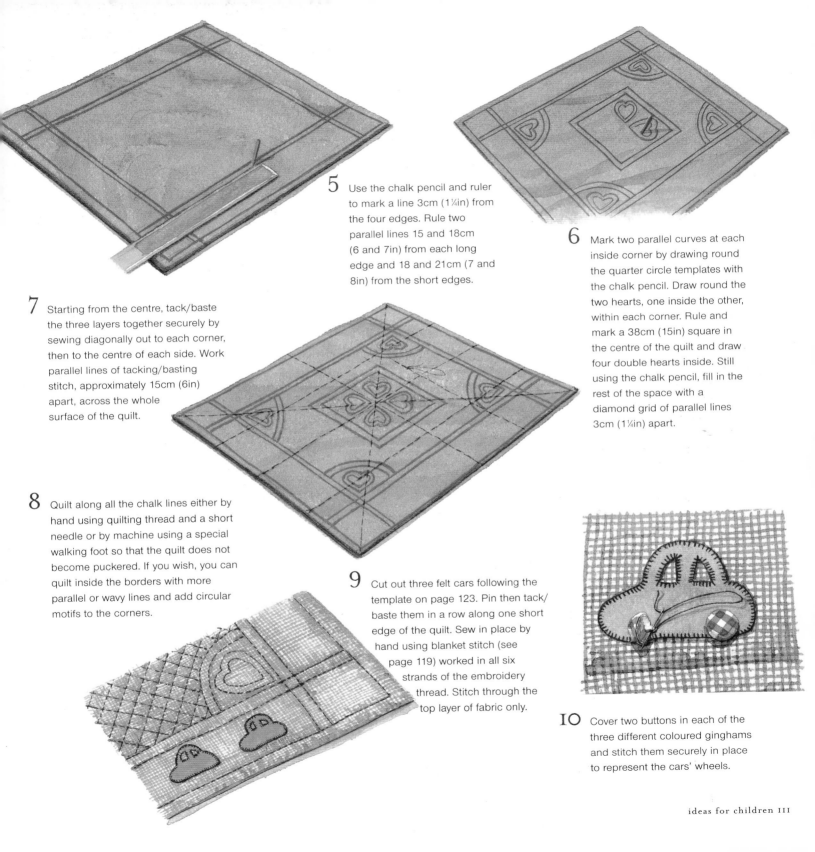

5 Use the chalk pencil and ruler
to mark a line 3cm (1¼in) from
the four edges. Rule two
parallel lines 15 and 18cm
(6 and 7in) from each long
edge and 18 and 21cm (7 and
8in) from the short edges.

6 Mark two parallel curves at each
inside corner by drawing round
the quarter circle templates with
the chalk pencil. Draw round the
two hearts, one inside the other,
within each corner. Rule and
mark a 38cm (15in) square in
the centre of the quilt and draw
four double hearts inside. Still
using the chalk pencil, fill in the
rest of the space with a
diamond grid of parallel lines
3cm (1¼in) apart.

7 Starting from the centre, tack/baste
the three layers together securely by
sewing diagonally out to each corner,
then to the centre of each side. Work
parallel lines of tacking/basting
stitch, approximately 15cm (6in)
apart, across the whole
surface of the quilt.

8 Quilt along all the chalk lines either by
hand using quilting thread and a short
needle or by machine using a special
walking foot so that the quilt does not
become puckered. If you wish, you can
quilt inside the borders with more
parallel or wavy lines and add circular
motifs to the corners.

9 Cut out three felt cars following the
template on page 123. Pin then tack/
baste them in a row along one short
edge of the quilt. Sew in place by
hand using blanket stitch (see
page 119) worked in all six
strands of the embroidery
thread. Stitch through the
top layer of fabric only.

10 Cover two buttons in each of the
three different coloured ginghams
and stitch them securely in place
to represent the cars' wheels.

When it comes to putting ideas into practice, you need only the most basic needlework skills to create your own cushions, pillowcases and throws. The following instructions will guide you through the techniques and equipment required for the step-by-step projects and show you how to make your own creations.

practicalities

SEWING KIT

THE EQUIPMENT AND HABERDASHERY/NOTIONS NEEDED FOR MOST SEWING PROJECTS IS MINIMAL, BUT IT IS WORTH INVESTING IN THE BEST POSSIBLE TOOLS TO HELP YOU ACHIEVE LASTING AND PROFESSIONAL RESULTS.

SEWING MACHINE

Modern machines have many advanced features, but for throws and cushion or pillow covers only a basic straight stitch and a zigzag for appliqué and neatening/finishing seams are necessary. Always use a sharp needle and match its thickness to the weight of the fabric: the finest ones have the lowest numbers, so use size 8 for fine cottons, size 12 for most projects and size 16 for heavy furnishing cloth.

SCISSORS

It is useful to have several different pairs of scissors, each kept for its own purpose:

• dressmaking shears with long blades are used for cutting out fabric and should be kept sharp. Do not use them to cut paper. The handles are bent at an angle so that they can cut accurately.
• sewing scissors are smaller and have straight handles. Use these for notching and trimming seams or corners.
• embroidery scissors have short, pointed blades, ideal for clipping thread and notching seam allowances.
• paper scissors should be kept specially for cutting out patterns and templates.

NEEDLES

Hand-sewing needles come in various sizes for different tasks. Medium-length sharps are best for general sewing and tacking/basting, while shorter ones can be used for slip stitch. Crewel needles have an extra-long eye designed for embroidery threads.

THIMBLE

A flat-top metal thimble should be used to protect the fingers when quilting and tacking/basting heavy fabrics together, although it may take a while to get used to.

DRESSMAKER'S PINS

These can be used for most fabrics, but larger glass-headed pins show up better on thicker material. Be sure to choose pins made from rustless steel.

SEWING THREAD

Always choose a thread made from the same weight and fibre as the fabric being stitched. Mercerized cotton has a smooth surface and should be used for cotton and linens. Polyester thread is finer and can be used for mixed fabrics. Match the colour of the thread as closely as possible to that of the fabric. Choose a darker shade if you can't find an exact match.

TACKING/BASTING THREAD

The loosely spun thread used for tacking/basting is not mercerized, which means it breaks easily and can be unpicked without damaging a finished seam. Use a contrasting colour that shows up well when tacking/basting stitches are to be removed.

MARKING TOOLS

The following marking implements make a useful addition to your sewing kit:

• tailor's chalk, which comes in a thin, solid block, produces a fine line that brushes away easily. Use white for dark fabrics and the coloured versions to mark paler cloth.
• chalk pencils can be sharpened to a fine point for detailed marking.
• dressmaker's pens have a water-soluble or light-sensitive ink which washes out or fades completely in a matter of hours without leaving any marks on the fabric.
• dressmaker's carbon paper is used for transferring embroidery designs. Lay a sheet onto your fabric with the shiny side facing down and fix down with low-tack masking tape. Tape the design on top and draw carefully over the outline with a sharp pencil.

IRON

Fabrics should be ironed before being made up and hems and seams need to be pressed well – so you need a good steam iron and a large ironing board. Use a cleaning cloth to remove any build-up on the iron and descale regularly. A dressmaker's sleeve board is useful for more intricate work.

MEASUREMENTS

Precise measurement is vital, so obtain a good tape measure that will not stretch with use and become inaccurate. Always follow either the metric or the imperial measurements when making a project.

PLAIN SEAM

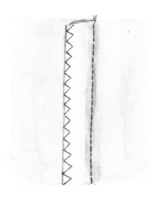

NEATENED/FINISHED SEAM

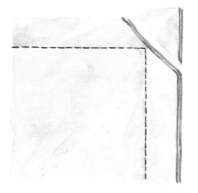

SEWING ROUND
A CORNER

FLAT FELL SEAM

FRENCH SEAM step 1

FRENCH SEAM step 2

SEAMS AND HEMS

IF YOU CAN HEM THE EDGES OF A LENGTH OF FABRIC AND JOIN TWO PIECES
TOGETHER, YOU HAVE MASTERED THE BASIC TECHNIQUES OF SEWING AND
SHOULD BE ABLE TO TACKLE ALL OF THE STEP-BY-STEP PROJECTS DESCRIBED
IN THE EARLIER CHAPTERS.

1 PLAIN SEAM

The extra fabric needed to join two edges is given as the seam allowance.
To keep the seam consistent, match the raw edges to the corresponding
line on the machine's baseplate when stitching. With right sides
together, line up the two edges and pin at 5–10cm (2–4in) intervals.
Tack/baste, then machine stitch along the seam line. Unpick the
tacking/basting, then press the seam open or over to one side, as
directed.

2 NEATENED/FINISHED SEAM

Raw fabric edges may fray, especially if an item is washed, but this can be
prevented by neatening/finishing the seam. If it is to be pressed open,
zigzag or overlock each cut edge before seaming. If the seam is to be
pressed to one side, the allowance can be trimmed and the two edges
zigzagged together (as shown in the diagram).

3 SEWING ROUND A CORNER

Stitch to the end of the seam allowance and, keeping the needle down,
raise the presser foot. Turn the fabric through 90 degrees and continue
sewing. Clip off the corner to within 3mm (⅛in) of the stitching before
turning through so that it will lie flat.

4 FLAT FELL SEAM

This seam shows on the right side as two parallel rows of stitches. With
wrong sides together, make a plain seam as in 1 above, then trim one
seam allowance to 6mm (¼in). Press under 3mm (⅛in) along the other
allowance and tack/baste the fold to the main fabric over the shortened
edge. Machine stitch close to the fold.

5 FRENCH SEAM

Used for joining lightweight or sheer fabrics, a French seam encloses the raw edges completely. With the two wrong sides together, make a plain seam (see 1, left) 8mm (⅜in) from the edge of the fabric. Trim the seam allowance back to 6mm (¼in). Fold the fabric so that the right sides are now together and the first seam is covered (see Step 2, opposite, below right). Make a second seam, this time on the wrong side of the fabric, 8mm (⅜in) from the edge. Press the seam allowance to one side.

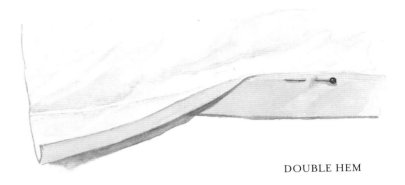

DOUBLE HEM

6 DOUBLE HEM

This consists of one narrow and one deeper turning or two equal-sized turnings (which give a firmer edge to finer fabrics). Press the two folds under and pin, then tack/baste in place. Machine stitch close to the inner fold or finish by hand with slip stitch (see 8, below) if you do not want the stitching to show on the right side.

7 MITRED CORNER

When two hems meet at right angles, the surplus fabric is neatened/finished with a mitre to prevent the corner from being too bulky. Press the turnings for the hems under on both sides, then unfold. Fold the corner inwards at a 45-degree angle and press so that the creases line up to make a square (as shown in the diagram, right). Refold, pin and tack/baste the hems, then slip stitch the folded edges (see below) before sewing down the seams. For a double hem, unfold the second turning only before refolding and stitching.

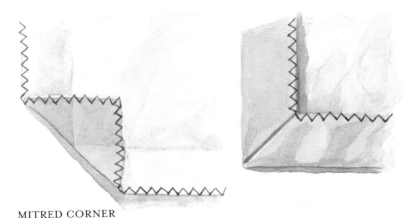

MITRED CORNER

8 SLIP STITCH

Slip stitch is used for joining two folded edges where they meet, for example, at a mitred corner or along the opening of a simple cushion cover and also to secure a double hem. Bring the needle out through the fold and pick up two threads of the other fabric on the other side with the point. Pass the needle back through the first fold for 6mm (¼in) and repeat to the end.

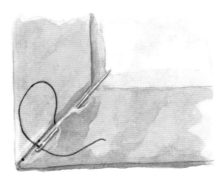

SLIP STITCH

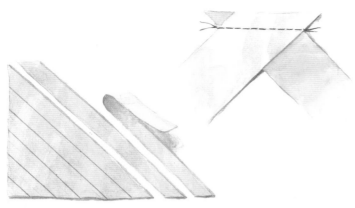

MAKING BIAS STRIPS

COVERING THE CORD

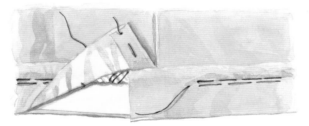

JOINING A ROUND OF PIPING/CORDING

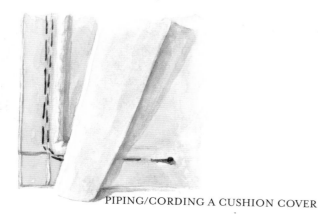

PIPING/CORDING A CUSHION COVER

PIPING/CORDING

PIPING — SOFT COTTON CORD COVERED WITH A BIAS FABRIC STRIP — IS USED TO REINFORCE THE SEAMS OF A CUSHION COVER AND TO DEFINE ITS SHAPE.

1   MAKING BIAS STRIPS

Mark a line across the fabric at a 45-degree angle to the edge. Draw a series of lines parallel to this and the same width as each other, then cut along the lines. With right sides together, sew the strips together at right angles to one another, 1cm (½in) from the edge, until you have reached the required length. Press the seams open.

2   COVERING THE CORD

With the right side outwards, fold the strip in half over the cord and pin, then tack/baste the two sides together 3mm (⅛in) from the cord.

3   JOINING A ROUND OF PIPING/CORDING

Tack/baste the piping/cording onto the main fabric, matching the raw edges. Leave a 2.5cm (1in) overlap at the join. Unpick the tacking/basting for 3cm (1¼in) at each side and trim the cord so that the ends butt up against each other. Stitch them loosely together. Tack/baste under the raw end of one strip and fold it over the other end to conceal the join. Tack/baste the unstitched piping cord down, then fit a zip foot to the sewing machine and stitch it in place, sewing close to the cord. If you are piping/cording a bolster cushion, line the join up to the main seam to make it appear less obvious.

4   PIPING/CORDING A CUSHION COVER

Pin and tack/baste the piping/cording to the right side of the first panel, matching the raw edges. The join should lie in the centre of one side or very close to a corner. Clip into the seam allowance of the bias strip at each corner to within 3mm (⅛in) of the cord so that it will turn neatly at a right angle. With right sides together, pin the second panel in place and complete as described for the basic cushion cover, opposite.

CUSHIONS AND PILLOWS

READY-MADE PADS/FORMS TO GO INSIDE CUSHIONS OR PILLOWS, WITH FEATHER OR SYNTHETIC FILLINGS, COME IN A MANY SHAPES AND SIZES.

1 BASIC CUSHION COVER

The simplest covers are closed with slip stitch. This has to be unpicked and resewn for cleaning, but it is almost invisible, especially if the seams are piped/corded. Covers should be the same dimensions as the pad/form, without any extra seam allowance, to give the cushion a well-stuffed look. Cut two pieces of fabric the same size as the pad/form. Add piping/cording if required (see page 116), then pin and tack/baste the edges together with right sides together. Machine stitch, leaving a 25cm (10in) gap along one side. Clip the corners, turn right side out and press. Press under the unstitched seam allowance. Insert the pad/form and slip stitch the opening with matching thread.

2 ENVELOPE BACK

This is made from two overlapping pieces of fabric. The opening can be left plain or embellished with ties or buttons. Cut the front panel to the same size as the pad/form. The two back panels are the same depth as the pad/form. Divide its width by two and add 13cm (5in) to find their width. Make a narrow double hem along one long edge of each panel. Lay the front face upwards and, matching the raw edges, place the two panels over it so that the hems overlap. Pin, tack/baste and stitch around all four edges. Clip the corners, turn right side out and press, then slip the pad/form in place.

3 BUTTONED FASTENINGS

If you want to add a row of buttons to an envelope back, the opening will need to be reinforced, so allow a 5cm (2in) double hem along each edge (see page 115). Mark the button positions along the centre of one hem and make matching vertical buttonholes on the other panel by hand or by machine. Make up the cover as described in 2, above, pinning on the buttonhole panel first, then sew on the buttons.

BASIC COVER step 1

BASIC COVER step 2

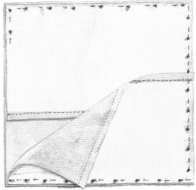

ENVELOPE BACK

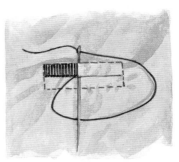

BUTTONHOLE

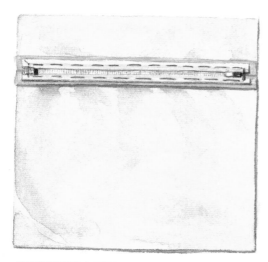

INSERTING A ZIP IN A PLAIN SEAM

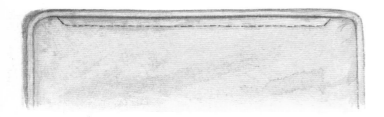

INSERTING A ZIP IN A PIPED/CORDED SEAM

BASIC PILLOWCASE

4 ZIPS

A zip makes a cover easy to remove but should be set close to one edge or into a piped/corded seam to make it inconspicuous. The zip itself should be 5cm (2in) shorter than the finished width of the cushion.

INSERTING A ZIP IN A PLAIN SEAM

Cut an 8cm (3in) strip the same length as the pad/form. Cut the main panel to the same length and 2.5cm (1in) less than the width. Neaten/finish the two edges that will be at either side of the opening. Tack/baste with right sides together, leaving a seam allowance of 2.5cm (1in). Make a 3cm (1¼in) seam at each edge, and work a few extra stitches at both ends to strengthen the seam. Press the seam open. Place the closed zip face down along the join. Pin and tack/baste both edges of the tape to the cover, then machine stitch close to the teeth, using a zip foot. Open the zip, unpick the tacking/basting and make up the cover as usual.

INSERTING A ZIP IN A PIPED/CORDED SEAM

Make a 3cm (1¼in) reinforced seam at each end of the side where the opening will be and neaten/finish the seam allowance. Undo the zip and, with right sides together, pin one edge centrally along the opening so that the teeth lie just beyond the piping/cording. Tack/baste and machine stitch close to the cord. Press the seam allowance to the wrong side and close the zip. Press under the other allowance and line the folded edge up with the piping/cording. Pin and tack/baste the second edge along the inside of the fold. Machine stitch 6mm (¼in) from the edge and across both ends. Join the other three sides of the cover.

5 BASIC PILLOWCASE

The traditional 'housewife' pillowcase is made with a deep tuck to hold the pillow securely inside the cover. For comfort and easy laundering, always make pillowcases from pure cotton or fine linen. The back panel is cut 2cm (¾in) larger all round than the pillow and the front panel is 20cm (8in) longer. Make a narrow double hem at one short end of each panel, then pin the raw ends together with right sides together. Fold the tuck back across the hemmed edge of the back panel and pin the sides together. Machine stitch leaving a 2cm (¾in) seam allowance. Trim and zigzag (or overlock) the seam allowance, turn right side out and press.

EMBROIDERY STITCHES

IF YOU WANT TO EMBROIDER YOUR CREATIONS, THERE IS A WEALTH OF STITCHES
FROM WHICH TO CHOOSE. HERE ARE SOME OF THE MOST USEFUL. FOR MORE
DETAILED DESIGNS, YOU CAN ADD BEADS, SEQUINS OR SEED PEARLS.

1 CHAIN STITCH

Re-insert the needle where it came up, looping the thread from left to
right. Bring it out over the loop, then re-insert at this point, making
another loop. Repeat to the end, anchoring the last loop with a short stitch.

2 DETACHED CHAIN STITCH

Also called lazy daisy, this stitch can be worked singly or in a circle to make
a flower. Insert the needle at the point where it came up and loop the thread
from left to right. Bring the point up over the thread and pull through.
Fasten the loop with a small straight stitch.

3 STEM STITCH

As its name suggests, this is the ideal stitch for flower stalks. Working from
left to right, make a straight stitch and bring the needle out halfway along
and to the left. Repeat, following the line of the design.

4 SATIN STITCH

Starting at the widest point of the outline, work series of diagonal straight
stitches, leaving no space between them, then fill in the remaining space.

5 CROSS STITCH

This can be worked singly or in rows. Make a diagonal stitch upwards from
right to left and bring the needle out directly below. Insert it again upwards
and to the right, making a second diagonal stitch across the first.

6 BLANKET STITCH

Traditionally worked in wool to neaten/finish the edge of woollen fabrics,
blanket stitch is also useful for outlines. Start on the lower line or the edge
of the fabric. Insert the needle up to the right and bring it out below with
the thread looped below the point of the needle. Continue working to the
right, and finish off with a short stitch over the final loop.

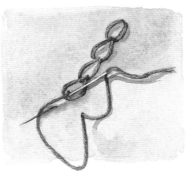

CHAIN STITCH

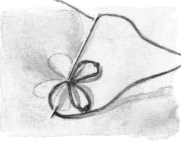

DETACHED
CHAIN STITCH

STEM STITCH

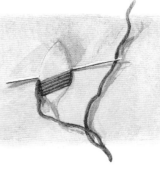

SATIN STITCH

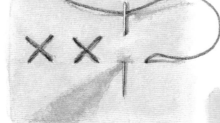

CROSS STITCH

BLANKET STITCH

templates

THE OUTLINES SHOWN ON PAGES 120–123 HAVE ALL BEEN REDUCED IN SIZE SO THEY FIT ON THESE PAGES. ENLARGE THEM ON A PHOTOCOPIER BY THE PERCENTAGES GIVEN TO MAKE THEM THE CORRECT SIZE.

ETHEREAL THROW (page 28)
ENLARGE BY 120%

ETHEREAL THROW (page 28)
ENLARGE BY 125%

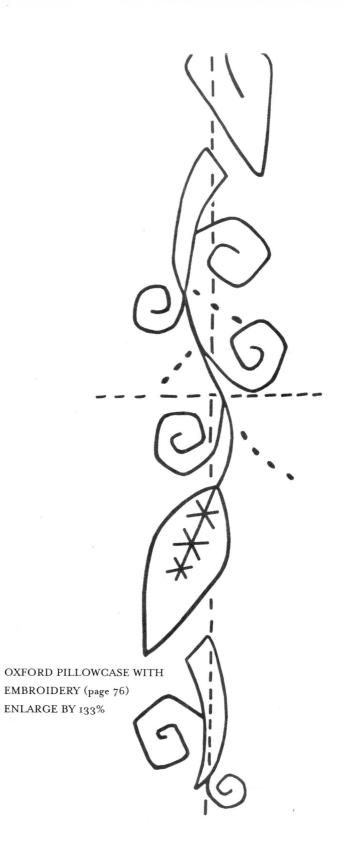

OXFORD PILLOWCASE WITH
EMBROIDERY (page 76)
ENLARGE BY 133%

GINGHAM QUILT (page 110) ENLARGE BY 125%

PYRAMID BEANBAGS
(page 106) ENLARGE BY 200%

GINGHAM QUILT (page 110) ENLARGE BY 125%

resources

THE COMPANIES LISTED BELOW SELL CUSHIONS, PILLOWS, THROWS, BED LINEN AND FABRIC IN ALL KINDS OF STYLES. CALL THEM OR VISIT THEIR WEBSITES FOR DETAILS.

UK

Cath Kidston
+ 44 (0)20 7221 4000
www.cathkidston.co.uk
Vintage florals and prints in contemporary style.

Colefax and Fowler
110 Fulham Road
London SW3 6HU
+ 44 (0)20 7244 7427
www.colefax.com
Classic, timeless fabrics.

Couverture
188 Kensington Park Road
London W11 2ES
+ 44 (0)20 7795 1200
www.couverture.co.uk
Original home accessories and unique bed linens, including a special range for children.

Designers Guild
267 & 277 Kings Road
London SW3 5EN
+ 44 (0)20 7351 5775
www.designersguild.com
Furnishing fabrics from over 50 collections.

Graham & Green
4 Elgin Crescent
London W11 2HX
+ 44 (0)20 7243 8908
www.grahamandgreen.co.uk
Home accessories.

Habitat
+ 44 (0)645 334433
www.habitat.net
Good value ready-made cushions and throws.

Heal's
+ 44 (0)20 7636 1666
www.heals.co.uk
Contemporary fabrics and soft furnishings.

Ian Mankin
109 Regent's Park Road
London NW1 8UR
+ 44 (0)20 7722 0997
www.ianmankin.com
Tickings, felt and utility fabrics.

Ikea
+ 44 (0)20 8208 5600
www.ikea.co.uk
Large range of soft furnishings.

J & M Davidson
42 Ledbury Rd
London W11 2AB
+ 44 (0)20 7313 9532
www.jandm-davidson.co.uk
Bed linens and home accessories.

Jane Sacchi
+ 44 (0)20 7351 3160
www.janesacchi.com
Antique and reproduction French linen and table linen, cushions, checks and ticking.

Jardin Provençal
6 Lostwithiel Street, Fowey
Cornwall PL23 1BD
+ 44 (0)1726 833762
Antique French linen and accessories.

John Lewis
+ 44 (0)20 7828 1000
www.johnlewis.com
Department store with more than 25 branches nationwide.

MacCulloch & Wallis
25–26 Dering Street
London W1S 1AT
+ 44 (0)20 7629 0311
www.macculloch-wallis.co.uk
Ribbons, trimmings and fashion accessories plus fabrics and sewing equipment.

Marimekko
16–17 St Christopher's Place
London W1U 1NZ
+ 44 (0)20 7486 6454
www.marimekko.co.uk
Bold, colourful and graphic prints from Finland.

Melin Tregwynt
Tregwynt Mill, Castlemorris
Haverfordwest
Pembrokeshire SA62 5UX
+ 44 (0)1348 891225
www.melintregwynt.co.uk
Traditional wool blankets.

Mulberry
171–75 Brompton Rd
London SW3 1NF
+ 44 (0)20 7838 1411
www.mulberry.com
Classic country style with a modern twist.

The Pier
+ 44 (0)20 7637 7001
www.pier.co.uk
Cushions and throws from around the world.

Sasha Gibb
+ 44 (0)1534 863211
Contemporary soft furnishings made from vintage blankets.

VV Rouleaux
6 Marylebone High Street
London W1M 3PB
+ 44 (0)20 7224 5179
www.vvrouleaux.com
Ribbons, trimmings, braid, couture flowers.

The White Company
+ 44 (0)870 900 9555
www.thewhitecompany.com
Traditional bed linen.

USA

A. C. Moore
+ 1 866 342 8802
www.acmoore.com
Craft superstore with over 70 branches.

Anthropologie
+ 1 800 309 2500
www.anthropologie.com
Vintage-inspired home accessories including bedspreads, pillows, and throws.

Barneys New York
+ 1 212 886 1199
www.barneys.com
Fine bedding and other home accents from this quality department store.

Bed, Bath & Beyond
+ 1 800 462 3966
www.bedbathandbeyond.com
One-stop shopping for contemporary home furnishings and accessories.

Bedside Manor
+ 1 800 485 4744
www.bedsidemanorltd.com
Fine blankets, bedspreads, linens and other bedroom accessories.

Calico Corners
+ 1 800 213 6366
www.calicocorners.com
Over 100 retail outlets discount a wide range of fabrics, buttons, trims and select seconds.

Crate & Barrel
+ 1 800 996 9960
www.crateandbarrel.com
Home accessories for contemporary living.

Gump's
135 Post Street
San Francisco, CA 94108
+ 1 800 882 8055
www.gumps.com
Luxury home furnishings and accessories.

Hancock Fabrics
+ 1 662 844 7368
www.hancockfabrics.com
Everything you need for projects involving sewing or fabrics.

Ikea
www.ikea.com
Large range of home furnishings.

Jo-Ann
+ 1 800 525 4951
www.joann.com
Craft supplies for all projects.

Laura Ashley, Inc.
www.lauraashley-usa.com
Cotton fabrics with English garden look. Coordinated pillows, bedding and trims.

Linen 'n' Things
+ 1 866 568 7378
www.lnt.com
Fabrics and home accessories.

Lowe's
+ 1 800 445 6937
www.lowes.com
More than 1,500 home improvement stores nationwide.

Michaels
+ 800 642 4235
www.michaels.com
Specialty retailer of arts and crafts items.

Pierre Deux
+ 1 888 743 7732
www.pierredeux.com
French country fabric and upholstery.

Pottery Barn
+ 1 800 922 5507
www.potterybarn.com.
Modern furnishings and home accents.

Rosebrand Textiles
4 Emerson Lane
Secaucus, NJ 07094
+ 1 800 223 1624
www.rosebrand.com
Muslin, scrim, ticking and other fabrics.

Salsa Fabrics
PO 193, Pleasant Valley Road
Spring Creek, NV 89815
+ 1 775 577 2207
www.salsafabrics.com
Original fabrics in cotton, silk and wool imported from Guatemala and Indonesia.

Takashimaya
693 Fifth Avenue
New York, NY 10012
+ 1 212 350 0100
www.ny-takashimaya.com
This Japanese department store features exclusive bedding and other luxury items.

Textile Arts
PO Box 3151
Sag Harbor, NY 11963
+ 1 888 343 7285
www.txtlart.com
Marimekko fabrics by mail order.

Urban Outfitters
+ 1 800 282 2200
www.urbanoutfitters.com
Trendy and playful home accessories.

West Elm
+ 1 888 922 4119
www.westelm.com
Modern home accessories in a zenlike style.

business credits

DESIGNERS, SHOP-OWNERS AND ARCHITECTS
WHOSE WORK IS FEATURED IN THIS BOOK

An Angel At My Table
14 High Street
Saffron Walden
Essex CB10 1AY, UK
+ 44 (0)1799 528777
also at:
537 Lisburn Road
Belfast BT9 7GQ, UK
www.anangelatmytable.com
Painted furniture and accessories.
Pages 30, 43al, 48, 55b, 81al,
85a, 87.

Blakes Lodgings
+ 1 631 324 1815
www.blakesbb.com
www.picket.com
Pages 72l, 78l.

Christopher Leach Design Ltd
Interior Designer
+ 44 (0)7765 255566
mail@christopherleach.com
Page 11al.

Coskun Fine Art London
+ 44 (0)20 7581 9056
www.coskunfineart.com
Page 11ar.

Emily Medley
Designer
emilymedley@mac.com
Page 72r.

The Housemade
Sue West
Interior & Product Design
+ 44 (0)1453 757771
suewest@thehousemade.com
www.avaweb.co.uk/coachhouse.html
Pages 45b, 82a, 83.

IPL Interiors
25 Bullen Street
London SW11 3ER, UK
+ 44 (0)20 7978 4224
Page 42.

Jonathan Adler
465 Broome Street
New York, NY 10013, USA
+ 1 212 941 8950
www.jonathanadler.com
Page 92.

jwflowers.com
Pages 6ar, 16l, 17, 18, 26, 51, 53,
65bl, 74, 75, 108.

Karen Nicol Embroidery
+ 44 (0)20 8979 4593
www.karenicol.com
Pages 6b, 22b, 23, 27–29, 65br,
81ar, 88–91.

Karen Spurgin
Textile Designer
+ 44 (0)20 8355 4729
www.spurgin.co.uk
Page 6ar, 65bl, 74, 75.

Ken Foreman
Architect
+ 1 212 924 4503
Page 93al.

Lattika Jain
Freelance in Textile Design,
Fashion & Knitwear
+ 44 (0)20 8682 3088
Page 45b.

Laura Bohn Design
Associates, Inc.
+ 1 212 645 3636
www.laurabohndesign.com
Page 23.

Laurent Bayard
Interiors
+ 44 (0)20 7328 2022
Pages 16r, 31br, 34, 35, 39,
40, 96, 97.

Lisa Bynon Garden Design
+ 1 631 725 4680
Page 9al.

Mona Nerenberg
Bloom
+ 1 631 725 4680
*Home and garden products
and antiques.*
Page 9al.

Mullman Seidman Architects
Architecture & Interior Design
+ 1 212 431 0770
www.mullmanseidman.com
Page 93ar & b.

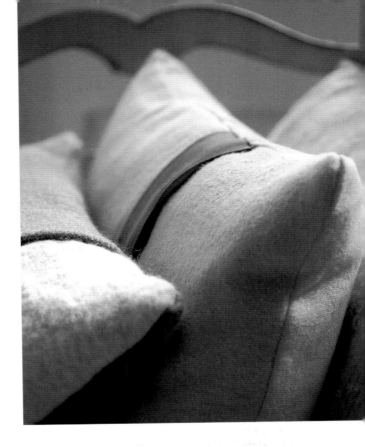

Pat Giddens
68 Golborne Road
London W10 5PS, UK
+ 44 (0)20 8964 1185
*Curtains, blinds and soft furnishings in
a modern Indian style.*
Pages 1r, 7, 26, 34, 35.

R. K. Alliston
173 New Kings Road
Parsons Green
London SW6 4SW, UK
also at 6 Quiet Street
Bath, Somerset BA1 2JS, UK
+ 44 (0)20 7751 0077
mail order: + 44 (0)845 130 5577
www.rkalliston.com
*An inspiring collection of practical and stylish
items for the garden and the home.*
Pages 12–15, 21ar, 84.

L'Utile e il Dilettevole
Via Carlo Maria Maggi 6
20154 Milan, Italy
+ 39 02 34 53 60 86
www.utile-dilettevole.it
Page 59b.

picture credits

ALL PHOTOGRAPHY BY SANDRA LANE UNLESS STATED OTHERWISE.

KEY: ph=photographer, a=above, b=below, l=left, r=right, c=centre

1l pillowcase from J&M Davidson, lavender bag from Graham & Green; 1c throw from Graham & Green; 1r cushion made by Pat Giddens; 2–5 Sophie Eadie's family home in London; 6al Hatty Lane-Fox's house in London – pillowcases and sheet from J&M Davidson, throw from The White Company; 6ar Paul Balland and Jane Wadham of jwflowers.com's family home in London – patchwork blanket from Daniela Besso, patchwork cushion made by Karen Spurgin; 6b Karen Nicol and Peter Clark's home in London – cushions and throws by Karen Nicol; 7 vintage cushion from Cath Kidston, mattress made by Pat Giddens; 8 cushions from Charlotte Casadejus; 9al ph Jan Baldwin/Mona Nerenberg and Lisa Bynon's house in Sag Harbor; 9b ph Jan Baldwin/Gabriele Sanders' Long Island home; 10 cushions from Charlotte Casadejus; 11al ph Jan Baldwin/Christopher Leach's apartment in London; 11ar ph Jan Baldwin/Art dealer Gül Coskun's apartment in London; 11br cushion from Mulberry; 12–15 Harriet Scott of R.K. Alliston's apartment in London; 12 & 13 pillowcases from Couverture; 14 & 15l throw from Muskett & Mazzullo, cushion by Double Helix Design; 16l Paul Balland and Jane Wadham of jwflowers.com's family home in London – pashmina by Mulberry; 16r Laurent Bayard's home in London – cushion from Muskett & Mazzullo; 17–18 Paul Balland and Jane Wadham of jwflowers.com's family home in London – linen throw made by Lucinda Ganderton; 20 ph Jan Baldwin/David Gill's house in London; 21al Robert Elms and Christina Wilson's family home in London – pillowcases by Megan Park; 21ar Harriet Scott of R.K. Alliston's apartment in London – throw and cushion from Couverture, mohair cushion from The White Company; 21b ph Alan Williams/Laura Bohn's apartment in New York designed by Laura Bohn Design Associates; 22l ph Jan Baldwin/ David Gill's house in London; 22b & 23 Karen Nicol and Peter Clark's home in London – floral throw and cushion from Graham & Green, sugared almond bolster made by Lucinda Ganderton; 26 Paul Balland and Jane Wadham of jwflowers.com's family home in London – patchwork cushions made by Pat Giddens; 27–29 Karen Nicol and Peter Clark's home in London – cushions and throw by Karen Nicol; 30 the home of Patty Collister in London, owner of An Angel At My Table – fringed cushion from The White Company, bolster vintage Cath Kidston at An Angel At My Table; 31al throw from Mimo; 31ar cushion from Couverture; 31bl pillowcases and throw from Graham & Green; 31br throw made by Laurent Bayard; 32 cushions from Couverture; 33 cushions and throw by Daniela Besso; 34–35 Laurent Bayard's home in London – cushions and throw from Mulberry, patchwork cushion by Pat Giddens; 36l ph James Merrell/Gabriele Sanders' apartment in New York; 36r–37 Robert Elms and Christina Wilson's family home in London – wool pillowcases and throw from Graham & Green; 38l cushion and throw from Mulberry; 38r throw from Mimo; 39–40 Laurent Bayard's home in London – throw made by Laurent Bayard; 42 ph Simon Upton/designed by IPL Interiors; 43al the home of Patty Collister in London, owner of An Angel At My Table – square cushions from An Angel At My Table, bag by Cath Kidston at An Angel At My Table; 43ar cushion from Graham & Green; 43b striped cushion, pale blue floral cushion and blanket from Cath Kidston, pink and turquoise floral cushions from Charlotte Casadejus; 44 & 45al Robert Elms and Christina Wilson's family home in London – cushions and throws from J&M Davidson; 45ar ph Polly Wreford; 45b ph Catherine Gratwicke/interior designer Sue West's house in Gloucestershire – cushion made by Lattika Jain; 46–47 Sophie Eadie's family home in London – pillowcases by Bleu; 48 square cushions from An Angel At My Table; 50r cushions from Jane Sacchi; 51 & 53 Paul Balland and Jane Wadham of jwflowers.com's family home in London – cushion from Jane Sacchi; 54 ph Catherine Gratwicke/Kimberley Watson's house in London; 55al Hatty Lane-Fox's house in London – velvet cushions from Graham & Green; 55ac ph Polly Wreford; 55b top left cushion from An Angel At My Table, all other cushions and throws vintage Cath Kidston at An Angel At My Table; 56 & 57al cushions and throw from Cath Kidston;

57ar ph Polly Wreford; 57br pink and turquoise floral cushions from Charlotte Casadejus; 58 & 59a cushions and throw from Une Histoire Simple; 59b ph Christopher Drake/Enrica Stabile's house, Le Thor, Provence – garden bench, cushions, watering can, tea cup & basket, l'Utile e il Dilettevole; 60l floral throw from Graham & Green; 60r ph Verity Welstead/ throws by Lulu Guinness; 61 ph Catherine Gratwicke/Lulu Guinness's home in London; 62 ph James Merrell; 64 Robert Elms and Christina Wilson's family home in London – cushions and throws by Megan Park; 65al cushion from Graham & Green; 65ar pillowcase made by Lucinda Ganderton; 65bl Paul Balland and Jane Wadham of jwflowers.com's family home in London – patchwork blanket from Daniela Besso, cushion made by Karen Spurgin; 65br vintage throw courtesy of Karen Nicol; 66 embroidered cushion and throw by Megan Park; 67–69 Robert Elms and Christina Wilson's family home in London – cushions and throws by Megan Park; 70b quilt, cushion and throw from Graham & Green; 70a & 71 embroidered cushions by Megan Park; 72l ph Alan Williams/Blakes Lodging designed by Jeanie Blake www.picket.com/blakesBB/blakes.htm – throw by Jeanie Blake; 72r ph Catherine Gratwicke/ Rose Hammick's home in London – French antique sheet awning Kim Sully Antiques, patchwork quilt by Emily Medley, bed from Litvinof & Fawcett; 73 cushions from The Pier, throw from Cath Kidston; 74 & 75 Paul Balland and Jane Wadham of jwflowers.com's family home in London – patchwork blanket from Daniela Besso, cushion made by Karen Spurgin; 76 pillowcase made by Lucinda Ganderton; 78l ph David Montgomery/Blakes Lodging designed by Jeanie Blake www.picket.com/blakesBB/blakes.htm – throw by Jeanie Blake; 80 cushions by Sasha Gibb; 81al the home of Patty Collister in London, owner of An Angel At My Table – bed and quilt from An Angel At My Table, pillowcase made by Lucinda Ganderton; 81ar cushion by Karen Nicol; 81b ph Catherine Gratwicke/Laura Stoddart's apartment in London; 82b ph Caroline Arber; 82a & 83 Catherine Gratwicke/Interior designer Sue West's house in Gloucestershire – selection of cushions on sofa made by Sue West, blind made from tea towel–style fabric from The Housemade; 84 Harriet Scott of R.K. Alliston's apartment in London – pillowcases from The Laundry, throw from Mimo; 85a toile cushions from An Angel At My Table, cashmere cushion from The White Company; 85b ph Caroline Arber; 86 & 87 the home of Patty Collister in London, owner of An Angel At My Table – bed and quilt from An Angel At My Table, pillowcase made by Lucinda Ganderton; 88–91 Karen Nicol and Peter Clark's home in London – all cushions made by Karen Nicol; 92 ph Catherine Gratwicke/Jonathan Adler & Simon Doonan's apartment in New York; 93al ph Alan Williams/An apartment in New York designed by Ken Foreman; 93ar & b ph Jan Baldwin/Peter & Nicole Dawes' apartment, designed by Mullman Seidman Architects; 94 fur throw from Interiors bis, geometric cushion by Double Helix Design; 95 ph Catherine Gratwicke /Francesca Mills' house in London – cushions from After Noah; 96–97 Laurent Bayard's home in London – throw and cushion from Liminal; 98 Robert Elms and Christina Wilson's family home in London – cushions from Graham & Green; 99–100 transfer print cushions made by Lucinda Ganderton; 102 ph Debi Treloar/Ben Johns & Deb Waterman Johns' house in Georgetown; 103al pillowcase from The Monogrammed Linen Shop; 103bl ph Debi Treloar; 103r–105l Sophie Eadie's family home in London; 103r strawberry cushions from The Cross; 105r & 106 Hatty Lane-Fox's house in London – pyramid cushions made by Lucinda Ganderton; 108 Paul Balland and Jane Wadham of jwflowers.com's family home in London – sleeping bag and striped cushions from Cath Kidston, cowboy cushion from Vintage Cath Kidston; 109a embroidered cushion by Ikea; 109b Hatty Lane-Fox's house in London – gingham quilt customised by Lucy Berridge, pillowcases from The Monogrammed Linen Shop; 112–113 ph Tom Leighton; 125 cushions by Sasha Gibb; 128 cushion from Couverture.

index

acknowledgments

This book is very much a joint creation by the art, editorial and production team at Ryland Peters & Small, and would not have been possible without their considerable skills. I would like to thank Alison for including me in the team; Sharon for her faultless editorial work and patience; Sandra and Lucy for creating the wonderful pictures and Claire for location research; Gabriella and Fiona for the overall look; Patricia for making it happen; and Lizzie for, once again, illustrating the projects so beautifully.

LUCINDA GANDERTON

I would like to thank everybody who lent the gorgeous cushions and throws featured in this book, without which the end result would not be as stunning as it is. Special thanks go to Lucinda Ganderton, Charlotte Casadejus and Pat Giddens for their exquisite work and generosity.

LUCY BERRIDGE